W9-BXT-229

THE MAD ISLANDS
and
THE ADMINISTRATOR

by Louis MacNeice

★

POETRY

The Burning Perch
Collected Poems, 1925-1948
Selected Poems
Eighty-five Poems
Visitations
Autumn Journal
Autumn Sequel
Ten Burnt Offerings
The Earth Compels
Springboard: Poems 1941–4
Holes in the Sky
The Other Wing
Solstices

★

DRAMA

The Dark Tower
Christopher Columbus
The Agamemnon of Aeschylus
(*translation*)

THE MAD ISLANDS
and
THE ADMINISTRATOR

Two radio plays

by

LOUIS MACNEICE, *1907-1963*

BRIAR CLIFF COLLEGE
LIBRARY
SIOUX CITY, IOWA

FABER AND FABER
24 Russell Square
London

First published in mcmlxiv
by Faber and Faber Limited
24 Russell Square London WC1
Printed in Great Britain
by The Bowering Press Plymouth
All rights reserved

PR
6025
.A316
M3
1964

© *1964 by Hedli MacNeice*

CONTENTS

INTRODUCTION

page 9

THE MAD ISLANDS

page 13

THE ADMINISTRATOR

page 73

5

43638

Introduction

These two plays were both written for what some think an obsolescent medium. Obsolescent or not, sound radio, in Britain at least, is not the *mass* medium it used to be, television having stolen most of its public though it cannot take over most of its territory. Sound radio can do things no other medium can and, if 'sound' dies, those things will not be done. So I offer these two plays in print not only as readable pieces (or I hope so) in their own right but also as specimens of a peculiar genus which may soon become a historical curiosity. In getting these pieces ready for print I have not altered the dialogue but have cut out the technical radio directions (the 'slow cross-fades', the 'hold behinds', etc.), and have substituted more intelligible signposts. On the other hand I have resisted the temptation to tag on many adverbial labels to the speeches, words like 'calmly', 'rapidly', 'disingenuously'; I like to think that these qualities are implicit in the lines. At the beginning of *The Mad Islands* I indicate that a harp was used: in fact it was used repeatedly throughout the production both to suggest changes of mood and place and to cover the passage of time; very often it was mixed with recorded effects, naturalistic or 'radiophonic', i.e. doctored.

The Administrator was written and broadcast in 1961, *The Mad Islands* in 1962. The two plays, though in many ways quite dissimilar, have certain things in common. First and most important, they are both essentially 'radio', i.e. with all their jumping about, whether in time or place and between the actual and the fantasy, they could not be anything else. Then they both, in a way, are studies in frustration. As regards the fantasy element, the dreams in *The Administrator* correspond to the islands in the other play. But here perhaps the difference between them is most important: the dreams in *The Administrator* are 'naturalistic' in that they are the kind those particular dreamers might have in 'real life'; they are also intended to throw light on both the characters and the pasts of the dreamers. In *The Mad Islands*, on the other hand, we never get *out* of fantasy and the 'characters' (see below) are barely characterized. But this does not mean

7

Introduction

(again see below) that *The Mad Islands* is a simple 'escapist' fairy story that has nothing to do with the world we live in.

Compared with plays written for the stage, works such as these may appear very bitty until you get used to them. I find myself that one of the attractions of radio is that you can move so fast, almost as fast as dreams do: this is why the medium is a good one for dealing with dreams and why, the other way round, a dream technique suits the medium. But a word of warning about 'symbolism', that old thing which makes so many people bristle: neither of these pieces is intended as *primarily* symbolic, at least in the narrow and *deliberate* sense (though in *The Mad Islands* certain hard-edged symbols are inherited), still less as allegorical, meaning one-for-one correspondence. But in both plays there is meant to be a good deal of *suggestion* and overlapping of references. Not only again is this very feasible in radio: as one's time is too often too limited, it *pays* to do several things at once.

The Administrator needs little comment: I had a compulsion to write it as this sort of painful choice seems endemic in our society. My chief trouble here was the ending. Originally I intended to end it with Jerry still not making up his mind but, being told that the listening public hated this, against my grain and the probability of his character made him follow his wife's wishes. I have now stood this decision on its head. *The Mad Islands* I wrote because I have always been addicted to the legendary Ancient Irish voyages which suggested it. In the original legend of Maeldúin *thirty-one* islands were visited. Alwyn and Brinley Rees in their book *Celtic Heritage* observe that in these voyages (the Voyage of Bran is another one) 'our world as we know it seems to resolve itself into its components', e.g. in an Island of Laughter people do *nothing but* laugh. I used one or two of the original islands and invented the others, just as Tennyson did in his 'Voyage of Maeldune', which he wrote in 1881 after reading P. W. Joyce's *Old Celtic Romances*, where the story was first published in English. One original motif which Tennyson ignored and I jumped at is that of the Miller of Hell, who in Joyce's version describes himself thus: 'I am the miller of hell. All the corn and all the riches of the world that men are

8

Introduction

dissatisfied with . . . are sent here to be ground, and also every precious article, and every kind of wealth, which men try to conceal from God. All these I grind in the Mill of Inver-tre-Kenand, and send them afterwards away to the west'.

Apart from adding and subtracting islands I also twisted the basic story line: the vendetta is traditional but not my dénouement. And the seal-women, though thoroughly Celtic and appearing repeatedly in Irish and Scottish folk-lore (see *The People of the Sea* by David Thomson), did not originally have anything to do with Maeldúin: the taboos, on the other hand, are traditional. Going wider, I did not mean my play to be either essentially Irish (in spite of its somewhat stylized dialogue) or consistently of the saga period. In fact half its point is its anachronisms. For this is something else that radio can get away with : a character can slip in and out of different periods without any embarrassment to himself or the listener. On the stage or the screen it would be highly embarrassing and not only in the little matter of costume.

L.M.

THE MAD ISLANDS

Main Characters [in order of appearance]
MULDOON, WHO HAS A QUEST
CORMAC, HIS FRIEND
THE JESTER
MULDOON'S MOTHER
URSACH, THE STEERSMAN
SKERRIE, THE SEAL-WOMAN
THE FUNSTER
BRANWEN AND OLWEN, THE RIVAL SISTERS
THE MILLER OF HELL
THE DROWNED MAN
THE QUEEN OF THE TWILIGHT
THE INVENTOR
THE HERMIT

'The Mad Islands' was first broadcast in the B.B.C. Third Programme on 4 April 1962. Details are as follows:

Muldoon	Denys Hawthorne
Foster-Brother and Friend	Barry Keegan
Jester	Billy Quinn
Mother	Eithne Dunne
Steersman	Rio Fanning
Seal Woman	Margaret Gordon
Funster	John Glyn-Jones
Branwen	Catherine Dolan
Olwen	Elizabeth Morgan
Miller of Hell	Brian O'Higgins
Drowned Man	Robert Mooney
Queen of the Twilight	Cecile Chevreau
Inventor	Richard Pasco
Hermit	Norman Wynne

Harp played by Osian Ellis
Special effects by the B.B.C. Radiophonic Workshop
Produced by Louis MacNeice

THE MAD ISLANDS

The play begins with harp music. Two young men are
playing chess in a big house in Ancient Ireland.

CORMAC: Your move, Muldoon.

[*Pause.*]

Your move I said, Muldoon.

MULDOON: My move?

CORMAC: Easy now—your king's in danger.

MULDOON: I can't see that.

CORMAC: Well, I've warned you.

[*After a pause a chessman is moved. Another pause and another*
is moved.]

CORMAC: Check!

MULDOON: Check?

JESTER: And mate.

MULDOON: Who asked you, fool?

JESTER: I know a mate when I see one. As the black
bull said when they offered him the nanny-
goat.

MULDOON: Is it mate, Cormac?

CORMAC: It is, Muldoon.

MULDOON: Why do I always lose at this game?

JESTER: Because chess is like life.

CORMAC: Quiet, fool!

JESTER: Look at this board. He need never have
lost the queen. The queen! Ha! Ha! The
queen!

[*Moving off.*] He could find her again if he
wanted to.

MULDOON: What did he mean by that?

CORMAC: Nothing. Talking like a fool is his business.

MULDOON: Why did you order him quiet then? I am of
age now. Tell me.

CORMAC: Yes, you are of age at last. All right then.
I didn't tell you before because you're my
foster-brother and I wouldn't be losing you
yet.

15

MULDOON: Why would you lose me at all? An orphan like me, I've nowhere to go.

CORMAC: The queen that was lost is still on the board. But she lives far away. A black queen, I reckon, or a red one.

MULDOON: Lay off the riddles.

CORMAC: I'm talking about your mother. She's still alive. We lied to you.

MULDOON: You lied! You all of you lied? My mother still alive! How do I know you're not lying now?

CORMAC: It was your mother sent you here. I was an infant then too so I cannot tell you the why or the wherefore. But my parents, who were alive then, she made them promise not to tell you. Not till you came of age.

MULDOON: Well, I am of age now.

CORMAC: Yes, at last, and that is why I am telling you. It is your move now, Muldoon.

MULDOON: Where does my mother live?

CORMAC: Far up the board to the north. Her knights and her bishops have all run away and her ivory castles are chipped. And the square she has moved to is black.

MULDOON: Do you know the way there?

CORMAC: My fool knows the way. Fool! Fool! Where are you?

JESTER: Yes, Cormac?

CORMAC: I have told Muldoon. Now we must take him to his mother. We leave at once, you must show us the quickest way.

JESTER: 'Never take a short cut', says the old proverb. And it's double true in a case like this. Bound for the heart of the blackest bogs of Ireland, running the gauntlet of the will-o'-wisps and the haunters, and then not knowing what we will meet at the end of it!

The Mad Islands

MULDOON: We will meet music.

JESTER: Meet what?

MULDOON: A long-lost mother is music.

JESTER: She might be. And she might not.

[*A great gong takes us to the long-lost mother.*]

MOTHER: There! I have only to strike this gong and you see how my whole house shakes. As if it would sink in the bog like the great beasts lived here once. But you—my only and long-lost son—am I not speaking for an hour and I have not shaken you at all!

MULDOON: But you have, mother, you have!

MOTHER: Then what are you waiting for? Why are you not on your way?

MULDOON: You have not kissed me yet.

MOTHER: I will—when you have done your mission. You say you have never been to sea?

MULDOON: No, mother. Only in dreams.

MOTHER: How do you mean 'only'? I have not seen the sea—or smelt it or felt it—for years. And yet once I lived in a castle with sea north, west, and south of it. Oh the braided brine and the grace-notes of the wind, the smell of the wrack and the company of gulls! But I could not go near the sea now, not while that man's alive and roving the western islands. Water is not like land, each drop links on to the next drop; there is never a break or a baulk in it. One driblet of foam on my foot or one wisp of spray in my face and I'd feel that murderer was touching me. So long as he is out there sailing it, the whole of that sea is defiled. It is for you to make it pure again.

MULDOON: With blood you mean, mother?

MOTHER: With blood. But, landlubber that you are, I will have to loan you a steersman.

The Mad Islands

[*She raps the gong twice, sharply.*]

URSACH: You sounded for me?

MOTHER: I did. Ursach, I am sending you to sea again.

URSACH: To sea?

MOTHER: You do not look pleased.

URSACH: My death will come from the sea.

MOTHER: Is it worse than a damp bed with the rats scrabbling in the thatch? After all you are a steersman.

URSACH: My hand and the tiller are long since parted.

MOTHER: This is my son Muldoon.

URSACH: Your son but——! Are you Muldoon?

MULDOON: I am, Ursach, and I need you. Will you steer me around the western seas till. . . .

URSACH: Till what?

MOTHER: Till you find the killer of his father.

URSACH: Is it you have set him on, Finoola?

MOTHER: Who else?

URSACH: Who else! If you asked *me*, Muldoon——

MOTHER: No one is asking you.

MULDOON: I *am* asking him something. Is it true that he killed my father?

URSACH: Oh, that part is true.

MULDOON: Very good. Mother, that knife on the wall—may I have it from you as a keepsake?

MOTHER: That was the knife that did it. I found him in the church with that in his heart. Take it and make good use of it.

URSACH: A knife gives a simple answer. Just one jab and it is tit-for-tat. But when I try to weigh things up——

MOTHER: Who asked you to weigh things up? Muldoon, repeat what I have told you.

MULDOON: My father, your husband, was murdered by his friend. Stabbed in the back while he was praying in church. Just a day and a night before I was born.

MOTHER: And the name of the friend? The title, I should say.

MULDOON: He is known as the Lord of the Eskers. He is now a sea-rover in the west. This being so, I must go to the Port of the Unwise and build or buy me a boat which Ursach here will steer.

URSACH: If I consent.

MOTHER: You will.

MULDOON: For this boat I will raise a crew, seventeen men neither more nor less; one more or less and ill luck will follow. Cormac, will you be one of them?

CORMAC: What do you think?

MULDOON: And you, fool?

JESTER: I might as well. A fool is always at sea.

MULDOON: Thank you. That is two. And you, Ursach?
[Pause.]

URSACH: Make it three.

MOTHER: I knew you were loyal, Ursach.

URSACH: I am loyal to this man for the sake of his father. I would not have him lost among the islands.

MULDOON: Are there so many islands?

URSACH: No man yet has counted them.

MOTHER: But at one or the next you will find the Lord of the Eskers. And when you have found him, what then?

MULDOON: With this very knife that killed my father——

MOTHER: You will strike him, my son. Like this!
[She strikes the gong very loudly. Its reverberations melt into the bustle of a quay. Muldoon is assembling his crew.]

MULDOON: Ursach, how many have we now?

URSACH: Sixteen. We need one more.

JESTER: They may call this the Port of the Unwise but I think the unwise men in it have all signed up already.

URSACH: If we had the one more we could sail on the tide.

CORMAC: Look, Muldoon! There's someone coming now. Coming down over the slippery stones, moving like a dancer through the slime and the seaweed. There's great balance and poise for you.

MULDOON: He's coming this way. Maybe he wants to join us.

URSACH: He, Muldoon? It's a woman.

JESTER: And a strange woman at that. Look at the round head on her and the way the hair lies close to it.

URSACH: There'll be no women in *my* crew!

CREW: No! That's right! A woman would bring bad luck.

[*Their anger and superstition simmer.*]

MULDOON: *Your* crew, Ursach? It's I give the orders here.

URSACH: Then you can find another steersman.

[*The strange woman joins them, unperturbed by their threatening aspect.*]

SKERRIE: Good day to you all. I heard you were a man short.

MULDOON: But you're not a man.

SKERRIE: Nor quite a woman either.

MULDOON: Meaning by that?

SKERRIE: I leave you to guess.

URSACH: Just leave us anyway!

[*The anger of the crew has now come to the boil.*]

CREW: That's right! Off with you! [*Etc.*]

MULDOON: Be quiet, all of you! What is your name?

SKERRIE: Skerrie they call me.

MULDOON: That's an odd name.

JESTER: It goes with the big eyes on her.

URSACH: There's a rock near Orkney called the Sule Skerry. It's known for the seals that breed there.

The Mad Islands

SKERRIE: Aye, there are quite a few seals there. I come from those parts, you know. But I know these seas well too, I've been round a number of the islands; there's not one island among them the same as the one before or after. Now the first island we shall come to——

URSACH: *We* shall come to!

SKERRIE: The first island we shall come to is the Island of Foolish Laughter. But we must put out at once or we shall miss the tide.

URSACH: It will mean bad luck if we take her.

CREW: That's right. Bad luck! Bad luck!

URSACH: Where does this island lie, woman?

SKERRIE: West-north-west from the Rock of the Oratory. It is thirteen leagues and a bit. You cannot mistake it for the crowds of birds on it.

URSACH: She does know these seas, it seems.

MULDOON: Better than you do. We take her.

[*They take her. And the sound of harp and oars takes all of them out to sea.*]

SKERRIE: Your steersman is still angry with me.

MULDOON: He thinks you are not a right woman.

SKERRIE: Has he never heard of the Children of Lochlann?

MULDOON: I dare say not. I haven't myself.

SKERRIE: To whom it is given that our land-longing shall be sea-longing and our sea-longing shall be land-longing. So that we are never satisfied.

MULDOON: Why have you come with me, Skerrie?

SKERRIE: I have not yet told myself why.

[*The harp and oars cover a passage of time.*]

LIAM: Land! Land ahead! To starboard!

URSACH: Land ahead, Muldoon!

MULDOON: Is this right?

SKERRIE: It is the island I told you of.

MULDOON: Right, Ursach. Steer straight for it.

SKERRIE: The Island of Foolish Laughter. Here you must go ashore and ask for the Lord of the Eskers.

MULDOON: You will not come with me?

SKERRIE: That is not allowed. Go only yourself and Cormac and the Jester.

MULDOON: And who will I ask about the Lord of the Eskers?

SKERRIE: There is only one man to ask. You see, Muldoon——

JESTER: Muldoon! Muldoon! Will you look at that island! It's fly-blown!

SKERRIE: Those are not flies.

JESTER: What are they then?

SKERRIE: Birds, man. Laughing birds.

[*The harp gives way to a chorus of birds laughing.*]

FUNSTER: Thank you, my feathered friends. Now let me tell you another. A funny thing happened to me on my way to this island this evening.

[*The birds laugh still more.*]

MULDOON: Forgive me. May I speak to you?

FUNSTER: Not till I've finished my act.

[*The birds continue laughing.*]

On my way to this island this evening——

[*The bird laughter increases again.*]

I met a Gael and a Gall. The Gall said to the Gael 'How are you blowing, my lord?'

[*The birds are now laughing themselves silly.*]

The Gael replied: 'My lord, I find your questions too galling.'

[*The birds think this the funniest thing ever but gradually their laughter subsides.*]

Thank you, my feathered friends. You may have heard it before but it's none the worse for that.

JESTER: I think it stinks.

The Mad Islands

FUNSTER: Who are you, sir?

JESTER: Just someone who knows about laughter.

FUNSTER: In that case you are a trespasser. Have you a permit for laughter?

JESTER: A permit?

FUNSTER: A permit, a pass, a diploma——

JESTER: I am a fool, like my father before me. And I got my first laugh when I was in the cradle.

FUNSTER: Well, you won't get any laugh here.

MULDOON: Stop this argument. What I want to ask is——

JESTER: So I won't get a laugh here?

FUNSTER: This audience has certain standards.

[*One or two birds squawk to show that they take the point.*]

You can try though, if you like.

JESTER: Thank you. I will. Watch me. Eagles, puffins and loons, razor-bills, wild geese and kittiwakes, ravens, sea-ravens and cormorants—— I am now going to make you laugh. If I don't you may give me the bird.

[*Silence.*]

Oh. Well, let's try again. Ah, just the story for you lot. Once upon a time there was a wren, a robin and a Jew——

[*Silence.*]

And they met in the middle of a holly-bush——

[*Silence.*]

You can keep this audience. They're deaf.

FUNSTER: Listen, my friend. If you want to make people laugh——

MULDOON: Listen to *me*. It's a matter of life and death. You must see everyone that comes to this island?

FUNSTER: Naturally.

MULDOON: Then have you seen—or heard of—the Lord of the Eskers?

FUNSTER: Is that a riddle? I know some too. What happens when you step on the horizon?

JESTER: It's like putting your hand up a skirt. You know that you've gone too far.

FUNSTER: What happens when you come to the end of a rainbow?

JESTER: You meet the smiling face of the tax man.

FUNSTER: What happens when you dig up a fairy mound?

JESTER: A fairy mound. Well, I hardly like to tell you——

MULDOON: Stop wasting the time. The Lord of the Eskers?

FUNSTER: Never heard of him. What's his speciality?

MULDOON: He killed my father.

FUNSTER: So that's his speciality. Did you hear that, my feathered friends? This gentleman's looking for someone who killed this gentleman's father.

[*The birds begin laughing again.*]

That's what I said, my feathered friends. He killed this gentleman's father. Well, you can't go farther than that.

[*The birds once more laugh themselves sick; then their laughter dissolves into the harp and the sounds of a boat at sea.*]

SKERRIE: The next island is the Island of the Rival Beds.

MULDOON: Whose rival beds?

SKERRIE: Branwen's and Olwen's—they're sisters. And here you must be very careful. For here you must go ashore alone.

MULDOON: Why must I go ashore at all?

SKERRIE: The Lord of the Eskers is fond of women. Of all the islands he might well choose this one. But, when you meet these two sisters, be sure you do nothing but question them. Will you promise me that?

MULDOON: I promise you.

[*The harp music fades and there is silence; and then the love-cry of a tom-cat.*]

BRANWEN: Conor! Out you go!

OLWEN: That is no way to treat him.

BRANWEN: I can't bear it when he stares at me like that.

OLWEN: It reminds you, does it, Branwen?

BRANWEN: He was a marvellous lover.

OLWEN: I could have had him if I'd wanted.

BRANWEN: You could not, Olwen. But I could have had your grey one there.

OLWEN: That's not true; is it, Diarmid?

[*Diarmid miaws.*]

OLWEN: He says No, you see.

BRANWEN: He says Yes—don't you, Diarmid?

OLWEN: Hsh, there's someone coming.

BRANWEN: It's a man!

OLWEN: Yes, a man—for the moment, poor thing. What are you doing, slipping your dress off the shoulder?

BRANWEN: And what are *you* doing, shaking out your hair like that?

OLWEN: Hsh!

BRANWEN: Hsh yourself!

MULDOON: May I come in?

BRANWEN: You are welcome.

OLWEN: This is only a humble bower but——

MULDOON: Are you Branwen and Olwen?

BRANWEN ⎱
OLWEN ⎰ : We are.

OLWEN: Let me give you some wine.

BRANWEN: You are windblown. Let me comb your hair.

OLWEN: You look tired. Come and sit beside me here.

MULDOON: Thank you, but I'm in a hurry, I——

BRANWEN: In a hurry, man? Shame!

OLWEN: No one comes here in a hurry.

BRANWEN: And no one leaves in a hurry. [*Laughs.*]

OLWEN: Good for you, Branwen. No one leaves in a hurry!

[*Both laugh.*]

MULDOON: All I want to ask is——

BRANWEN: Why is your hand bleeding?

MULDOON: It was those cats outside.

BRANWEN: The wicked things! They would be jealous.

OLWEN: They ought to know better by now. We've tried to train them, you know, but——

MULDOON: Have you seen the Lord of the Eskers?

BRANWEN: Yes, we've tried to train them, but, you see, they're Irish.

OLWEN: We've only been here two years, you know.

BRANWEN: And haven't we a nice crowd of cats to show for it?

OLWEN: When we left the land of our fathers we meant to be back by sundown.

BRANWEN: We had hired such a pretty little boat—they said it was suitable for ladies—but indeed we never meant to go farther than Anglesey.

OLWEN: Suitable for ladies! We were carried away, man. Of course all our family have stormy natures.

BRANWEN: That's what our stepfather said. He called it the weather in the soul.

OLWEN: No, not the soul, the mind.

BRANWEN: Or was it the heart?

OLWEN: We're both wrong; it was the intestines.

BRANWEN: No, that wasn't the word. I think it began with a 'w'.

OLWEN: Or would it have been a 'v'? Well, never mind, we had a good blow for our money.

MULDOON: I'm sorry to keep asking questions. Have you seen the Lord of the Eskers?

OLWEN: You asked that already.

MULDOON: But you didn't answer.

BRANWEN: The Lord of the Eskers? What sort of man was he then?

OLWEN: Was he ginger with a bull neck?

BRANWEN: Was he wearing a furry grey cloak with black markings like a mackerel?

OLWEN: Or a black jerkin with snow-white gloves and boots?

BRANWEN: And what were his whiskers like? Did they stick out straight or did they droop?

MULDOON: I have never met the man.

BRANWEN: Well, when would he have been here?

MULDOON: A week ago—a month—a year—I couldn't tell you for certain.

BRANWEN: If you will come to my room, I will show you my list.

OLWEN: Come to mine. My list is longer.

BRANWEN: It is not.

OLWEN: It is. And I have little bells on my bed.

BRANWEN: She has too—but my bed is softer.

OLWEN: Her bed may be softer. When it comes to other things——

BRANWEN: Don't listen to her. The proof is in the meeting.

MULDOON: All I want to know is: if the Lord of the Eskers was here, when did he leave?

BRANWEN: Oh, he would not have left.

OLWEN: How could he?

BRANWEN: They never leave—and it costs us a fortune in milk.

OLWEN: You have probably seen him already.

BRANWEN: Maybe it was he that scratched you.

MULDOON: If you mean what I think——

OLWEN: You are very quick at guessing.

[BRANWEN *and* OLWEN *laugh.*]

OLWEN: Why did you want this Lord of the Eskers anyway?

MULDOON: To kill him.

BRANWEN: To kill him! Oh, you villain!

MULDOON: And, if you have turned him to a cat, I shall kill him just the same.

BRANWEN: You will do no such thing. We have never lost a cat yet.

OLWEN: Anyway you'd never guess which he was.

MULDOON: Make me a cat too and I'll soon know which he is.

OLWEN: We will not make you a cat!

BRANWEN: Quite right, Olwen. And we won't even let him go to bed with us.

OLWEN: Certainly not. And what's more we'll deport him from the island.

BRANWEN: Yes, that's what we'll do, we'll deport him! Brian, Fergus, Conor, the lot of you——

OLWEN: Diarmid, Feargal, Stumpy-Tail, the lot of you——

[*The cats begin gathering.*]

BRANWEN: Cats who used to have souls——

OLWEN: Cats who used to wear jerkins and breeches——

BRANWEN: Cats who used to go to church——

OLWEN: Cats who used to go to bed——

BRANWEN: Gather round all of you and out with your claws! Drive this man into the sea!

[*The cats hiss, spit, scream and snarl.*]

MULDOON: Keep back! Keep away! Or I'll kill you!

OLWEN: Look at him walking backwards, waving his little knife. He's afraid of our cats, Branwen.

BRANWEN: And well he might be, Olwen. They were all great fighters in their time.

OLWEN: Yes and they fought to kill. But the funny thing, Branwen, is this. This Lord of . . . Lord of . . .

BRANWEN: The Eskers.

OLWEN: He is one killer that never came here— worse luck.

The Mad Islands

[*The cat noises fade and the harp comes back and* MULDOON *is out at sea again.*]

SKERRIE: It was my mistake, Muldoon. I was told so while you were on shore. The Lord of the Eskers never landed on that island. He was swept clean past it by a storm.

MULDOON: Who told you that?

SKERRIE: An old acquaintance of mine. He was just passing by.

MULDOON: Rowing or sailing?

SKERRIE: Swimming. And he told me the Lord of the Eskers is just one jump ahead of us. Maybe even at that next island we're coming to.

MULDOON: Which island is that?

SKERRIE: It belongs to the Miller of Hell.

[*Out of nowhere comes the noise of a water mill, with a crowd swarming around it.*]

MILLER [*stentorian*]: One at a time there! One at a time! Rotten oats on the left, mildewed barley on the right! And mind you don't fall down the shaft with them! Come along there, walk up, I'll buy all your doubts and disappointments, your defeated hopes, your encumbrances, I'll buy all your chares and your chores, your backbitings and your second thoughts. Come on up there, shovel them in—your hypocrisies and mediocrities, your outmoded ornaments and armaments, your half-baked lumps of dough, your half-formed castles in the air, your stillborn babies, your unhappy pasts. Hurry up there, roll them all in, down the shaft with them, my mill's still hungry. Bring me your vows of eternal love, your oaths on the book, your questions of principle. Whatever you pretend to or no longer believe and whatever you believe mistakenly, whatever you have failed to do and whatever you have done to no purpose, whatever you think you are when you're not and whatever you are when you are—bring it all up and shovel it in, it's grist to my mill and to hell with it!

[*Pause.*]

You there! What have you in the sack?

MERCHANT: Gold.

MILLER: Pure gold?

MERCHANT: Stolen gold.

MILLER: That will do; tip it in. And what about you with the patch over your eye?

ONE-EYED MAN: What about me?

MILLER: What have you brought to be ground? Not a sack nor even a wallet, not a crate nor even a casket, not a sheaf of corn nor an ear of it——

ONE-EYED MAN: The patch on my eye.

MILLER: The patch? Is it no use to you?

ONE-EYED MAN: No use at all. Nor the eye underneath it.

MILLER: Then they're both for me—and my mill's still hungry. First the patch, my friend! That's the way. Now throw the eye after it. There! Don't you feel better? Now then! What about the other eye?

ONE-EYED MAN: I can still see middling with it.

MILLER: Only middling? Go on! Throw it in!

BUSYBODY: You do what he says. He'll grind it up new for you.

ONE-EYED MAN Here goes then!

[*He screams in agony.*]

BUSYBODY: Did it hurt?

ONE-EYED MAN: Oh the pain! The pain! And the darkness!

BUSYBODY: You'll get them back, you know, both of them. Or I should say all three of them: the two eyes and the patch. Just wait till they've gone through the mill.

FUNSTER: Make way there! Way for the lady! She has brought you something you'll like.

MILLER: And what is it this time, lady? A broken promise, a lying letter, a stolen trinket, a cuckolded husband——

FUNSTER: She's brought a cat in a bag.

MILLER: What's wrong with your cat?

BRANWEN: It's my sister's cat.

MILLER: A tom cat?

BRANWEN: Very much a tom cat.

[*The tom cat, from inside the bag, utters a muffled love call.*]

MILLER: Yes, I can hear he is. Very good, lady; down the shaft with him!

[*The love call changes to an anguished yelp.*]

BRANWEN: That will teach you to go to Olwen's room. Bells on her bed indeed! There'll be no more bells for you.

MILLER: And you, sir? Anything to grind? Don't keep me waiting, my mill's still hungry. Come on, sir, I know who you are. Any bad jokes today, any dirty stories? I remember now you brought me some before——

FUNSTER: No, nothing of that sort today. I am going the round of my properties. In fact I'm preparing for an auction.

MILLER: I know your auctions. Anything you don't sell, just ship it back here to me.

FUNSTER: I'll remember that but it may not take place for years. Time means nothing to me, you know.

MILLER: It doesn't to me much either. But then I'm the Miller of Hell.

FUNSTER: Well, come to my auction if you can. By the way, I saw two strangers round at the back by the mill race.

MILLER: Two strangers round by the mill race! They're not going to bathe in it, are they?

FUNSTER: If I were you, Miller, I'd go round and see.

MILLER: I think I will. I will not have people bathing in my sewage.

[MULDOON *and* CORMAC *go round to the back. There is no crowd here but the mill race is loud.*]

CORMAC: Will you look at that stream, Muldoon! Look at the scum there is in it. Where does it all go to?

MULDOON: I can tell you one thing, Cormac: seeing where the sun is setting, all that muck's flowing west.

MILLER: The sun here's always setting but you're right—it *is* flowing west. In fact it's flowing to hell and I am the Miller of Hell. But now I'll ask you two a question. What are you doing here, trespassing?

MULDOON: We are no trespassers. All we want is news.

MILLER: All news here is stale news. Can't you smell it?

CORMAC: We can!

MILLER: But, as stale news goes, I can offer you almost anything. Robbery, rape, arson, murder——

MULDOON: That last is the word. Have you seen the Lord of the Eskers?

MILLER: I have indeed. Not long ago.

MULDOON: How long ago?

MILLER: Five years maybe. Or again it might be ten or twenty.

MULDOON: Ten or twenty! You said not long ago.

MILLER: What is short to me might be long to you. I remember him well though; he brought me some stuff to grind.

MULDOON: I can guess what manner of stuff. An evil conscience, treachery, hatred, blood-guilt——

MILLER: No, nothing in that class at all. He brought

me a woman's handkerchief—embroidered
with flowers and small birds—and a woman's
gold bracelet and a necklace.

MULDOON: But I don't understand.

ONE-EYED MAN: My eyes! Where are my eyes?

MILLER: Eyes, man? What have you done with them?

ONE-EYED MAN: I gave them to you to grind and make new.

MILLER: You gave them to me to grind.

ONE-EYED MAN: But where are they?

MILLER: They've gone west, man.

ONE-EYED MAN: But I don't understand; they were to come
out new.

MILLER: None of you understand. I am the Miller of
Hell. What I take I take and it flows away
west. To the west, to death, to hell. And
none of it ever comes back again.

ONE-EYED MAN: Oh, I'm blind! . . . Blind! . . . Blind!

[*Out of the Dark Ages and the noise of the mill race come the
noises of a modern factory.*]

MILLER: There! What did you expect? This mill is a
going concern—expanding throughout the
centuries. Come on up, bring it in by the
crate, by the bale, by the waggon-load. I
will need new docks on this island, I will
need a dozen new docks. Come on, you fools
of the future, bring in your shiploads of folly.
All your bad debts and your crooked con-
tracts, your election speeches and your
changing maps, your mergers and treaties
and dud manifestoes, your flashy red herring,
your brand-new obsolescent weapons. Come
on up, roll it in, let me grind it away to the
west. Will you look at it now, my sewer's in
spate, it's goodbye to you all and the toil
of your hands, the filth in your guts and the
fraud in your hearts, it's goodbye to you all
and the seed of your loins. I will grind it

33

BRIAR CLIFF COLLEGE
LIBRARY

43638   SIOUX CITY, IOWA

away, grind it away, grind it away, grind it
away . . .

[*The* MILLER'S *voice, huge though it is, is drowned in hooters
and sirens. Then these in their turn recede and the sea takes
over again. It is colder now and no land in sight.*]

SKERRIE: We are coming now to more dangerous seas.
One ship out of three gets lost in them.

MULDOON: I cannot understand about the Lord of the
Eskers. A woman's necklace and a woman's
bracelet and a handkerchief embroidered
with——

URSACH: Birds and flowers.

MULDOON: Ursach! How did *you* know?

URSACH: A little bird told me—an embroidered one.

MULDOON: Ursach, you're keeping things back from
me.

CORMAC: Easy, Muldoon. Let the man get on with his
steering. Did you not hear what Skerrie said?

MULDOON: What did she say?

SKERRIE: I was only giving a warning.

[*Seals are heard lamenting in the distance.*]

MULDOON: What's that noise ahead of us? Who are they
keening?

SKERRIE: I told you people get drowned here. They are
keening no one but themselves.

JESTER: It's a wet wake all right but the wetness is
not of the best.

CORMAC: How many seals are there huddled on the
rock there?

MULDOON: Steer in to that rock, Ursach.

URSACH: And have me wreck the boat!

SKERRIE: That rock goes down sheer. Let them all
back water as they come to it.

[*Ursach steers in, the seawash on the rock is heard.*]

URSACH: Back water now! Back water!

[*The seawash on the rock is loud but the barking of the seals
tops it.*]

The Mad Islands

SKERRIE: Do you hear them greeting us? Greetings to you too. Now be silent.

[*The seals are silent.*]

Leave it to me now. I'll talk to them. You there. How long have you been drowned?

[*The first seal barks disyllabically.*]

Ten years he says. And you?

[*A second seal barks keeping the rhythm of the words.*]

'Twenty-one years come Easter.'
And you, old fellow with the limpets on your cheeks?

[*A third seal barks keeping the rhythm likewise.*]

He says he can't remember; it was before Christianity.

MULDOON: Why, there's a man among them. With his arms clasped round his knees. And shivering all the time, shivering. This is where I ask questions. Man, naked man, answer me! Why are you there among the seals?

DROWNED MAN: Because this is where I belong. I have been drowned too.

MULDOON: But you're not a seal.

DROWNED MAN: Not yet. I have been drowned too recently.

MULDOON: How recently?

DROWNED MAN: Only yesterday. My captain threw me overboard.

MULDOON: Why?

DROWNED MAN: Just out of pique. I told him he still had an eye for the women. So he pitched me out of the stern and now I am cold till doom.

SKERRIE: Not till doom. Once you are changed you will be warm again.

DROWNED MAN: How do you know? Who are you?

SKERRIE: Never mind who I am. I know.

DROWNED MAN: I too had an eye for women but I never saw one like you.

35

The Mad Islands

MULDOON: What was your captain's name?

DROWNED MAN: If only I was warm I would take you walking on the sea. We would gather the flowers of the sea and——

SKERRIE: You will be warm when you're changed.

MULDOON: What was your captain's name?

DROWNED MAN: My captain? Had I a captain?

MULDOON: Was it the Lord of the Eskers?

DROWNED MAN: I can't hear what you say.

SKERRIE: Spare him. The change is beginning.

MULDOON: Where was your captain bound for?

DROWNED MAN: [Shivers and groans.]

LIAM: Saint Brendan protect us! Look at him!

CORMAC: Look at his legs. They're flippers!

JESTER: Look at his hands. They're flippers.

MULDOON: Quick, before you go; answer me. Where was your captain bound for?

SKERRIE: I will try for you. Where was your captain bound for?

[The new seal barks.]

The Happy Island, he says.

JESTER: The Happy—— I'll believe it when I see it.

MULDOON: Skerrie, ask him one last——

SKERRIE: I will ask him no more at all. When this first happens they suffer.

CORMAC: God between us and evil! Look at his eyes, he's weeping.

SKERRIE: He makes a beautiful seal.

MULDOON: Sit to your oars, all of you! Ursach!

URSACH: Yes, Muldoon?

MULDOON: Steer for the Happy Island!

SKERRIE: Goodbye, drowned man, goodbye. You will be warm again soon.

[They leave the seals behind and hold on their course.]

MULDOON: Now tell me about this Happy Island.

SKERRIE: It is not really happy. Yet no one who lands there wants to leave there.

The Mad Islands

MULDOON: But I must land there.

SKERRIE: You must. If that man's captain was the Lord of the Eskers, he should be now with the Queen of the Twilight.

MULDOON: The Queen of——

SKERRIE: She is the one you must call on. But the more of you go, the more will be tempted, so here once again you must travel alone. The Queen lives inland behind cobweb curtains. Pay no heed to the people on the way there and above all don't take anything they offer you. If you do, you will become like them.

[*The next thing we know,* MULDOON *is on the island being tempted.*]

THE TEMPTERS: You look tired, stranger. Will you take a rest?
You look hungry, stranger. Will you take an apple?
You look thirsty, stranger. Will you take some ale?

MULDOON: I will not. Where has the sun gone?

TEMPTER: Where has the what gone?

MULDOON: The sun in the sky. It is morning.

THE TEMPTERS: It is never morning here.
There is never a sun in the sky.
Our queen does not like sunlight.

MULDOON: Your queen! Where is your queen?

THE TEMPTERS: In the birch-grove there.
In her house with the cobweb curtains.
As you go through them, do not break them.
Her spiders took years to spin them.
They are very beautiful cobwebs.
Are you sure you will not take an apple?
Or a peach? Or a plum? Or a cherry?
Or ale? Or wine? Or sleep?
Never mind. Our queen will give him some.

[*And so he moves on to face the* QUEEN.]

QUEEN: Have you ever seen an apple like this?

MULDOON: I have not.

QUEEN: Yet you still will not take it?

MULDOON: I will not.

QUEEN: But you will drink?

MULDOON: I will not.

QUEEN: Very well. We must make do with talk.

MULDOON: What will we talk about?

QUEEN: Me.

[*She waits for him to speak.*]

Well? Have you nothing to ask me?

MULDOON: Have you always lived here?

QUEEN: No.

MULDOON: Where did you come from then?

QUEEN: I have forgotten. But I remember one thing. Where I once lived there was a horror in the sky.

MULDOON: What kind of horror?

QUEEN: Something that hurt the eyes. It would hide behind the horizon and then it would jump up shouting and it would climb up the sky and all the flowers would open. And the brittle little birds would sing.

MULDOON: Are there no birds here?

QUEEN: They stay in their nests. And the flowers stay snug underground. That is why everyone is happy.

MULDOON: Because nothing ever happens?

QUEEN: Nothing ever happens. So everyone who comes here stays here. Just as you will, you know.

MULDOON: I will not.

QUEEN: You deceive yourself. Only one man came here who left again.

MULDOON: And when was that?

QUEEN: Just yesterday. Or was it the year before yesterday? But he was stronger than you.

The Mad Islands

MULDOON: How do you know?

QUEEN: He was the Lord of the Eskers.

MULDOON: Who?

QUEEN: Do you know him?

MULDOON: He killed my father.

QUEEN: I would have wished him to stay. He too liked the twilight.

MULDOON: The twilight! Do you see this knife?

QUEEN: Pretty. Where does it come from?

MULDOON: Out of my father's heart.

QUEEN: The nice thing about that Lord of the Eskers: he had neither past nor future.

MULDOON: His past was this knife—and his future is this knife.

QUEEN: He was happy while he was here. Did I offer you anything to drink?

MULDOON: You did. I refused.

QUEEN: That's funny. He refused too. But then he was stronger than you. So you really want to know where he has gone?

MULDOON: I do.

QUEEN: Then all you have to do is take this little apple——

MULDOON: I can't.

QUEEN: Just one little bite and I'll tell you.

[*Pause.*]

Just one little strip of the peel.

MULDOON: And then you will tell me?

QUEEN: Of course.

MULDOON: If I thought I could trust you——

QUEEN: But you can!

MULDOON: In that case . . . Hand me the apple.

[*Out of the distance, all the way from the sea, comes the voice of* SKERRIE, *but distorted now and harsh like that of a seal.*]

SKERRIE [*calling*]: Muldoon! Muldoon!

QUEEN: What was that? That horrible noise!

[*The distorted voice still penetrates.*]

The Mad Islands

SKERRIE: Muldoon! Come back to me! Come back!

[MULDOON *suddenly realizes his danger.*]

MULDOON [*calling back*]: Skerrie! I'm coming! I'm coming!

[*Pause.*]

QUEEN: He's gone. Two in two days! But look—he's torn my cobwebs! The webs it took years to spin! And what's that coming through my doorway? Stay away, stay away, keep out! No, don't come near me, don't touch me! I am the Queen of the Twilight, this is no place for you. This is my house, you can't come in here. Oh, it's coming, it's streaming in, it's flowing to my feet, it's probing—it will kill me, whatever it is—but I know what it is, I have met it before, it's the sun!

[MULDOON *has rejoined his boat, which is again in mid-sea.*]

MULDOON: Why did you call me back then?

SKERRIE: Muldoon! Look into my eyes.

MULDOON: Your eyes are always so sad?

SKERRIE: The tide in them stays at the full. There is only one element for people like me.

[*They suddenly hear a foghorn.*]

URSACH: What is that noise? Did you ever hear the like of that?

CORMAC: It must be some great sea-monster.

[*The foghorn sounds again—nearer.*]

JESTER: He should be more careful of his vocal chords.

LIAM: Yes, it's a monster all right.

SKERRIE: It is not. It is a foghorn.

[*The foghorn is joined by others. Soon there is a forest of foghorns.*]

URSACH: She's right. That fog came quickly.

MULDOON: Easy now! Look out for rocks!

URSACH: Slow there! Go slow! Your souls to the devil, we're aground.

SKERRIE: It's only a sandy beach. What they call the Beach of the Crucibles.

The Mad Islands

MULDOON: And the island itself?

SKERRIE: The Island of Progress. The whole of it, heather and rock, belongs to one man; he's an alchemist. If the fog were not so thick, you could see the smoke from his chimney; there is no smoke like it in the world.

MULDOON: He's the next I have to see, is he?

SKERRIE: He lives behind bolt and bar; to enter you need the password.

MULDOON: And what is the password?

SKERRIE: Today it would be . . . Tetragrammaton.

MULDOON: Tetra—what?

[*The password itself jumps him on to the island and there is the* INVENTOR *asking for it.*]

INVENTOR [*from behind*]: The password! The password!

MULDOON [*outside*]: Tetragrammaton.

INVENTORY: Wait till I let you in.

[*Bolts and bars are drawn back, a creaking door opens and closes:* MULDOON *enters the material laboratory.*]

INVENTOR: Now we haven't much time. Have you brought the ingredients?

MULDOON: The ingredients?

INVENTOR: Keep going over there with the bellows. As I said in my letter, I have plenty of mercury; also of sulphur and arsenic. But you know what I ordered: I have the list here. The gall bladder of a baboon, a quart of Dead Sea water, a sprig of withered mistletoe, and a pound of this new stuff—uranium.

MULDOON: I think there must be some mistake.

INVENTOR: Nonsense, I told you all this in my letter. I take it you *can* read Syriac?

MULDOON: Syriac? I haven't a word of it.

INVENTOR: Ah, that explains it. I wrote it in Syriac for safety. Everyone's so mad for gold, you know. But now that you're here you may as

> well see what goes on. Come and take a peep
> in the cauldron.

[*The cauldron bubbles as a slave works the bellows.*]

INVENTOR: There! Pretty colour, isn't it?

MULDOON: What colour do you call that?

INVENTOR: Yellow.

MULDOON: Would you now? I'd call it colourless.

INVENTOR: Oh, nonsense, sir, you must be blind. You'll
see what I mean if you taste it.

MULDOON: But I can't, it's too hot, it's boiling.

INVENTOR: Why, can't you drink things boiling? Then
you'll have to take my word for it: it's
almost *aurum potabile*. Almost but just not
quite. It's potable already but not yet gold—
not yet. When it is, I'll put up a notice: All
Gold to be Consumed on the Premises. You
know what the premisses are, of course?

MULDOON: Well, they seem rather draughty, or should
I say monastic——

INVENTOR: The first premiss is this: at the centre of
everything is nothing. Take, for example,
this block of granite; I lugged it all the way
from the beach, I'll pop it in the cauldron
shortly. Now you, being a layman, no doubt
would call this stone solid.

MULDOON: I might.

INVENTOR: Well, it's nothing of the sort. There are
more winds blowing through this single
stone than you'd find in the whole cave of
Aeolus. Now these winds couldn't blow at
all if they had no space to blow in. Space—
room for experiment. But for what kind of
experiment? You'll be surprised when I tell
you. This could make or break the world.

[*Someone outside hammers on the iron door.*]

> Perhaps that will be the ingredients. Who's
> there?

The Mad Islands

MILLER [*outside*]: A friend.

INVENTOR: Password then, friend?

MILLER: Tetragrammaton.

INVENTOR: Right. I won't be a minute.

[*The great door opens and the* MILLER *enters. Then the great door once more closes.*]

MULDOON: If it isn't the Miller of Hell again!

MILLER: Are you the nuclear alchemist? I heard your soup wanted colouring.

INVENTOR: It's not just the colour, you know; don't let us confuse cause and effect. Once we have achieved our transmutation of the primal matter——

MILLER: I have brought you a gallon of my best.

INVENTOR: Of your best what?

MILLER: Never mind. Just pour the whole lot in your cauldron.

INVENTOR: Take it, slave. Pour it in the cauldron.

The SLAVE *takes it and pours it. The cauldron reacts like a geyser.*]

SLAVE [*Screams*]: Oh, my foot! My foot!

INVENTOR: The clumsy fellow! He's scalded himself. Why have you gone over there into the corner?

MULDOON: I can't bear the smell.

INVENTOR: But it's the smell of progress! And the colour's *really* changing this time. Yellow? It's as yellow as buttercups. Do just come and see what's happening in the cauldron.

[*Out of the bubbling of the cauldron come the tickings and hummings of modern technology.*]

MULDOON: I'm watching what's happening in your room. Your filthy, black walls turning white, lights in great tubes in the roof, everything polished and shining and purring, rows upon rows of discs of crystal—some green, some red, some blue, some purple—

43

and in each of those discs a ticking needle—
tick, tick, tick!—you can hear them growing.
Growing! Growing like a cancer!

[*The tickings and hummings increase.*]

INVENTOR: News from the centre! Something out of
nothing! I have split the stone and released
the wind! I have split the wind and released
the whirlwind. Aurum potabile! Look!
Yellow—yellower—yellowest! Come over
here, both of you!

[*The* SLAVE *groans and falls with a thud.*]

MILLER: What's wrong with your slave?

INVENTOR: He's fainted. The fumes of the gold were too
much for him.

MILLER: Fainted, man? He's dead. Have you a large
sack?

INVENTOR: What for?

MILLER: Why, to take him away.

[*There is a violent noise as the caudron boils over.*]

INVENTOR: Oh, my God! The cauldron's boiling over.

[*And once again from the far distance is heard the strange cry,
half seal, half human.*]

SKERRIE [*calling*]: Muldoon! Muldoon!

INVENTOR: Don't open that door.

[*But he does. And, for the second time, he escapes like a flash.*]

INVENTOR: He's gone. And at such a moment! No
~~interest in science. Just think what he's~~
missing!

[*There is a violent explosion then the sound of falling debris:
then silence.*]

MILLER [*calmly*]: 'Science'? More grist to my mill then. Now
what did I do with that sack?

[*He prepares to dispose of the remains. But* MULDOON,
back at sea, sails on.]

SKERRIE: So all that time you never put your question!
You would not be forgetting your mission of
vengeance?

MULDOON: I would not.

SKERRIE: If you only did . . .

[*Pause.*]

MULDOON: Did you say something?

SKERRIE: When a man keeps his eyes on a target of hate the power to love goes out of him.

MULDOON: Ursach! I think I see land.

URSACH: You're right, Muldoon.

JESTER: Just another barren island?

URSACH: Not this time, fool. There's a big crowd of people there. All gathering outside a big building.

JESTER: Needless to say they call at this island too. Just in time for an auction. The auctioneer is someone they have met before.

FUNSTER: Thirty—I am offered thirty—thirty pieces of silver. Any advance on thirty? All done at thirty.

[*Gavel.*]

Sold for thirty pieces of silver. To the gentleman in the mask. Now my next lot, lot 99, is rather a mixed bag. I might call it a lot and a half or maybe a lot and a wife. It consists of the following items: one pillar of salt——

[*Laughter.*]

I thought I'd get a laugh on that. One pillar of salt, two turtle doves—No, I'm slipping, it's the other way round. Lot 99 consists of the following:—

[*Sings.*] Twelve bulls a-roaring,
Eleven cows swooning,
Ten commandments missing,
Nine ninepins falling,
Eight pimps a-pimping,
Seven stars a-sinking,
Six days a-working,
Five gold teeth,

Four talking fish,
Three mocking birds,
Two turtle doves, and
An old salt in a night dress.
The reserve price is one mess of pottage.

BIDDER: Two messes of pottage.

MILLER: One pot of sewage.

CORMAC: Him again!

OLWEN: One black tom cat two hands high.

BRANWEN: One black tom cat three hands high.

JESTER: And them again!

BIDDERS: One black wolfhound.
One black wolf.
One black gelding.
One black stallion.
One black centaur.

JESTER: One black snowball.

[*Pause.*]

FUNSTER: I am offered one black snowball. Any advance on one black snowball?

BIDDERS: One pack of cards you cannot lose with.
One great looking glass not to be looked in.

OLWEN: One little bed with bells on it.

MILLER: One great millstone to wear round your neck.

BIDDERS: One book of truth—both home and foreign.
One book of lies—both black and white.

BRANWEN: One book for bedtime.

JESTER: One book of Kells.

FUNSTER: One book of Kells. I am offered one book of Kells.

[*A tolling bell is heard.*]

Excuse me, here we must break off for the nonce. The bidding for Lot 99 rests at . . . one book of . . .Kells. But the next lot, I fear, is priority. There are two kinds of auction, as you probably know, the common and the extreme. Lot 99 is an instance of common. Extreme auction is when someone's dying. This is the case with lot 100. Hand me my hat with the weepers. Thank you. Lot 100, ladies and gentlemen, is dying at this moment in the centre of Ireland. She is of advanced years but has been well preserved in hatred. She has not one grey hair on her head nor, even on her deathbed, one tear in her eye. She has caused in her time a great deal of trouble: an excellent collector's piece. Any offers—while there's time—to save this woman's life? One of the great ladies of our day—her name, I'm afraid, is a secret—and not a grey hair on her head. She has plenty of venom in her yet—prolong her life and add a chapter to the annals of Ireland. Any offers for this life which is ebbing away every second. The reserve price is the life of the bidder.

[*Pause.*]

MULDOON: What did you say her name is?

FUNSTER: I am not allowed to tell you.

MULDOON: And where did you say she lives?

FUNSTER: In a bog in the centre of Ireland.

MULDOON: And you really may not divulge her name?

FUNSTER: No. But I can let you talk to her.

MULDOON: Talk to her?

FUNSTER: That's me. Always some new entertainment. Look behind you. See that little door in the rock?

MULDOON: That looks as if it had never been opened?

FUNSTER: It hasn't as yet. It leads to a small cold cell. There you will find a conch hanging from a golden rope. You must put that conch to your ear and wait till you hear what comes to you. Then speak into a hole

The Mad Islands

you will see in the wall. Provided it's working, a voice should come back to you.

MULDOON: Out of the conch?

FUNSTER: Out of the centre of Ireland.

[*A familiar gong is heard, but distorted as though by a weird
telephone.*]

MOTHER: Is there no one in this house? Answer me!
Have you all run away the first time I
really need you? Ursach! Where's Ursach?
No; I sent him to sea with my son. It's so
long ago I had forgotten. Me that had a
hundred servants to die here alone among
the rats!

MULDOON [*answering her from over the sea*]: Mother! Can
you hear me?

MOTHER: Who's that? A ghost?

MULDOON: Mother, this is me, Muldoon.

MOTHER: Then you're the ghost of Muldoon.

MULDOON: I am not, mother, I'm alive.

MOTHER: Where are you then?

MULDOON: On an island. And I can buy back your life.

MOTHER: Buy back my life! With what?

MULDOON: With my own life, mother.

MOTHER: With your own? Have you killed the Lord
of the Eskers?

MULDOON: No, I have not yet found him.

MOTHER: Not found him? After all this time?

MULDOON: Mother, I will bid for your life.

MOTHER: You will not. You still have your mission.

MULDOON: You prefer that I live to kill him?

MOTHER: Muldoon, my son, I am standing where you
first saw me. The first and last time you saw
me. I am standing unaided with the gong-
stick in my hand. I have only the strength to
strike it the once—— Let the sound of it
boom in your mind for ever. You have only
one thing to do: find that man before he dies

48

and, when you have found him, raise your right hand so and——

[*He hears a great blow on gong; then silence.*]

FUNSTER: The blessing of God on the souls of the dead. And now to return to Lot 99 . . .

[*On this note they leave the Island of the Auction. Back at sea, some spiritual stock-taking begins.*]

JESTER: The funny thing is: I don't own the Book of Kells.

URSACH: It's a good thing he didn't bid for her. This story is twisted enough as it is.

CORMAC: Stop muttering there. The wind's getting up. Muldoon, why don't you speak?

SKERRIE: Leave him to me. Muldoon, you couldn't have saved her. As a person dies his nature comes uppermost. Your mother's nature was not to be saved. Can you knit a shirt of spindrift or scutch the Milky Way!

MULDOON: My quest makes no more sense.

SKERRIE: It never did. Are you tired of the mad islands?

MULDOON: Tired!

SKERRIE: Very well then. I know quite a different island——

MULDOON: No, Skerrie, no! Don't tempt me. Your voice is a voice but it is not a gong.

SKERRIE: Muldoon, before it's too late—I am losing the best of both worlds——

MULDOON: Ursach! How are we doing?

URSACH: We are in for a storm, Muldoon.

MULDOON: Good. That suits my mood. Come on, you winds and waves!

SKERRIE: Be careful; they might hear you.

MULDOON: Come on, you endless waters! This is I, Muldoon, I dare you to drown me. Ha! You cannot drown me until I have killed. But where is the man I must kill? Where have you hidden him, winds and waters?

CORMAC: Muldoon! Sit down; you will fall overboard. Grab hold of him, Liam. And you too, Eamonn.

LIAM: Now then, Muldoon, if you'd just——

MULDOON: Let go of me or by the children of Lir——

[*In the struggle the two men fall overboard*].

MULDOON: Goodbye, Liam! Goodbye, Eamonn! Does anyone else feel like a dip?

[*The storm swells up. Somewhere a gong sounds through it.*]

MULDOON: It sounds in my mind . . . in the ruin of my mind. . . . It will sound for ever till that ruin falls.

[*The storm, as quickly, dwindles away again. The gong is heard again but farther off. We now hear the anguish of a steamship : their craft has suffered a sea change.*]

CORMAC: Am I imagining things or are we going much faster?

URSACH: Full ahead both.

[*Ting ting.*]

Starboard ten.

VOICE: Starboard ten, sir.

URSACH: Steer 268.

VOICE: 268, sir.

JESTER: Whether we're going faster or not, there's nothing, I always say, like a deckchair.

[*Pause.*]

SKERRIE: The wind's dropped.

MULDOON: Everything's dropped. Who are you? Where are we going?

SKERRIE: Who I am can wait. We're going to see a hermit. He lives on an island that's little more than a rock. He lives a life that is little more than a death. We must sound our siren to tell him we're coming. He is blind, you see, and all the great ocean is dark to him.

[*We now 'cut away' to this hermit.*]

HERMIT: Hos omnes invoco in auxilium meum. The

twelve youths who went with Columkill to
Alba. The seven holy bishops of the Church
of the Yew Wood. The seven holy bishops of
Tuam in Galway. The hermit found by
Brendan in the Land of Promise. Saint
Brendan himself on these cold seas before
me. Saint Brendan himself? . . . Saint
Brendan the Voyager.

[*A ship's siren is heard in the distance.*]

What is that new noise? I have never heard
it before. Hos omnes invoco in auxilium
meum.

[*The siren comes nearer.*]

Another temptation would it be? Is it from
hell this time or merely from the old gods of
Ireland? If only I had my sight! How long ago
was it the *last* monster came——

[*The siren is now very threatening.*]

And he roared no louder than that. And then
there was the time that the mermaids sang to
me—when I still had my sight and the other
thing. Even that temptation did not trap me.
But from that day on I reduced my diet—
God told me to.

[MULDOON *has now come ashore.*]

MULDOON: Stay here by the dinghy, the three of you. I
will go up myself and talk to him.

[*The* HERMIT *hears him from his higher position.*]

HERMIT: They're coming again—the demons. The
saints preserve me once more! Saint Michael
and his angels stand around me——

MULDOON [*from below*]: Father! Father, may I——

HERMIT: Demon! Don't touch me! In the name of the
Blessed Trinity——

MULDOON: I am no demon. I'm a man.

HERMIT: No men come here. You must prove it to
me. I'm blind.

MULDOON: Then you must take my word for it. I am a man, I swear it.

HERMIT: I need more than your word; they have fooled me before. Come up here and let me feel your body—a demon's body is cold, yet it makes one's fingers tingle. But, *if* you are a man, be careful; there is little room on this ledge.

[MULDOON *clambers up and joins him.*]

Are you here? Let me feel you.

[*The* HERMIT *passes his hands over* MULDOON's *body.*]

Yes, you have the pulse of a man. Where do you come from?

MULDOON: Ireland.

HERMIT: I come from Wales. But that was before you were born. Tell me: what do you see?

MULDOON: What do I see?

HERMIT: What do I look like to you? Do not lie to me.

MULDOON [*feeling for his words*]: You look . . . to me . . . like the oldest man in the world. Naked . . . a cage of bones . . . your face lathered with bog cotton.

HERMIT: But what do you read in my face?

MULDOON: There is so much hair I read nothing.

HERMIT: That is just as well. When I lived in the world I never stopped sinning. All the sins that there are except murder.

[*A seal, as it seems, barks in the distance.*]

Was that a seal? They come here rarely now. There is not enough for them to eat; the fish are few in these seas—as I knew when I still ate fish. All I live on now is limpets or winkles and seaweed. It is better, to keep down desire.

[*The seal barks again—nearer.*]

I think that seal means harm. What was I saying, my son?

The Mad Islands

MULDOON: Father, forgive me, I am pressed for time. For years that I cannot count I have been chasing a murderer. They call him the Lord of the Eskers.

[*There is a pregnant pause.*]

Father! What has happened? Where have you gone?

HERMIT: Say that again—the name of the man.

MULDOON: The Lord of the Eskers.

HERMIT: I never heard of him.

[*The seal barks—nearer still.*]

The bark of that seal makes me shiver. Oh for a fire—it is forty years since I saw one. But if I had a fire on this rock, I would never let it go out. And as each new night drew on —tell me, my son, is night coming now?

MULDOON: No, Father; it's high noon.

HERMIT: As night drew on I would rake the fire to preserve it and this is the prayer I would say: 'I rake this fire as the pure Christ rakes all. Mary at its foot and Brigid at its top. The Eight Highest Angels of the City of Grace preserve this house and its people till day!' I mean 'this rock and its hermit till day'.

[MULDOON *drops his dagger on the rock.*]

You dropped something. What is it?

MULDOON: Only a knife.

HERMIT: A knife? Let me feel it. I like the feel of a knife.

[MULDOON *is about to hand it to him but* SKERRIE *once again intervenes.*]

SKERRIE [*calling from the distance*]: Muldoon! Muldoon! Come at once!

HERMIT: There is that seal again.

MULDOON [*calling back*]: What is wrong, Skerrie?

SKERRIE: Come at once!

MULDOON: Forgive me, Father, I must go.

The Mad Islands

HERMIT: One moment, son. The knife!

[*There is a pause while* MULDOON *scrambles back down to the dinghy.*]

He has gone—and the knife with him. Mary, Queen of the Angels, Fountain of the Gardens, Star of the Sea, as the night falls, I rake this fire on the rock. The Eight Highest Angels of—Fire? But it's out! Mother of God, it's gone out!

[*A harp paints a ship becalmed and them on board her bemused.*]

URSACH: Muldoon, we are becalmed.

MULDOON: So is my will-power; the thrust is gone out of me.

SKERRIE: And it is time. Will I sing you a lullaby?

[*She croons something that suggests the Hebrides.*]

CORMAC: Muldoon! Muldoon! Look over the edge.

VOICES: Would you believe it!

The saints preserve us!

JESTER: The most beautiful town you ever saw. Glossy black cows in the streets, a white horse drawing a chariot——

MULDOON: What are you babbling about?

[*From below them they hear drowned bells.*]

SKERRIE: It is the Country-under-the-Sea.

MULDOON: I have often heard of that country. Perhaps we will get there some time.

URSACH: You can only see it when it's crystal calm. I have seen it twice but no good came of it.

CORMAC: Don't they all wear wonderful colours!

JESTER: And don't they all look very busy and brisk!

CORMAC: That's because they're going to church.

MULDOON: Church?

CORMAC: Can't you hear the bells?

MULDOON: I wish I was with them.

SKERRIE: Don't say that, Muldoon.

JESTER: I could look at this moving picture for ever.

The Mad Islands

That yellow-haired girl with the flowers in her pigtails! D'ye know, I think it's a wedding.

CORMAC: You're right. Those bells are wedding bells.

MULDOON: But why are they beginning to dance as they walk?

JESTER: Because they're happy, I suppose.

URSACH: That's no dancing, that's a ripple. Between them and us. Just the wisp of a gust.

CORMAC: He's right. Now they're walking steadily again.

[*Pause.*]

JESTER: Another ripple!

URSACH: The calm is ending.

MULDOON: No, stay! Stay there! Let me join you!

SKERRIE: You can't. Your time has not come.

JESTER: You can hardly see them now. Just a coloured blur. A blur!

MULDOON: Goodbye down there! God be with you!

URSACH: Get in the main sheets! The wind's rising.

[*There is a great flapping of sails and creaking of a wooden ship.*]

SKERRIE: So much for the Country-under-the-Sea. It is too late to escape, Muldoon.

MULDOON: Did I say I wanted to escape?

SKERRIE: You did not. I saw it in your eyes.

URSACH: Steer 155.

VOICE: 155, sir.

[*Suddenly, if unobtrusively, they are aboard a steamship.*]

JESTER: What I always say is: there's nothing like a deckchair.

[*Pause.*]

CORMAC: I don't know what's wrong with me. Fool, do you know what's wrong with me?

JESTER: Nothing, Cormac—except that you're going to die.

[*Pause.*]

URSACH: This tiller is no longer obeying my hand. This has never happened before.

SKERRIE: Everything has got to happen some time.

[*Pause.*]

SKERRIE: Don't you think so, Muldoon?

MULDOON: What?

SKERRIE: Everything has got to happen some time. But that time is fixed; you can never jump ahead of it.

MULDOON: I can jump ahead of it.

SKERRIE: How?

MULDOON: Ursach, where are we? How far from land?

URSACH: Two and a half leagues.

MULDOON: Then lower the gangway.

URSACH: I will not. Even if this tiller—but it isn't a tiller, it's a wheel.

MULDOON: What are you playing at? Lower the gangway!

SKERRIE: You are all at sixes and sevens. Where do you think you are?

MULDOON: *When* do you think we are?

CORMAC: I'm sorry, Muldoon, but nobody lowers a gangway in mid-ocean.

MULDOON: Oh, so nobody does? Then I'm nobody. I, nobody, alias Muldoon, hereby command my crew to lower the gangway and step on it. If Muldoon can't come to the island, then the island must come to Muldoon!

[*And so it does.*]

JESTER: But we don't want that island. Just look at it!

CORMAC: Where did all those people come from on the quay?

JESTER: For that matter, where did the bloody quay come from itself?

MULDOON: This is an order—Lower the gangway!

[*As the gangway is lowered the crowd on the quay become threatening.*]

56

CORMAC: Before you go ashore, Muldoon my foster-brother——

MULDOON: Yes, my foster-brother, what?

CORMAC: Those people don't look too friendly.

CROWD [*from the quay. Off*]: It's he! It's he! It's the very man! It's he!

MULDOON: You're right, they're pointing at me.

CORMAC: They seem to know you, Muldoon.

MULDOON: But I've never seen one of them before!

CORMAC: That could be because they have no faces.

SKERRIE: Muldoon, you mustn't go ashore.

MULDOON: Why not?

SKERRIE: I smell death in the air.

MULDOON: Then we will all take our weapons.

SKERRIE: No, no! Weapons will be fatal.

MULDOON: That's what they're for, Skerrie. And I don't want any more losses. We lost two good men not so long ago.

URSACH: *We* lost? *You* lost! Liam and Eamonn.

MULDOON: Silence, Ursach! Strap on your sword. And listen all of you! This time we all go ashore —except Skerrie. And we all go ashore fully armed.

[*They cheer and go clattering down the gangway.*]

CROWD: It's he! It's he! It's Muldoon!

MULDOON: Yes, it's I, Muldoon, and I'm coming!

[*He leads his crew down the gangway and in among the crowd on the quay. Not all in the crowd are new to us.*]

FUNSTER: Why, if it's not my old friend! Muldoon, my dear chap, have you heard this one?

MULDOON: I thought I left you at an auction.

FUNSTER: Yes and I lost my face there. But not— perish the thought—not, never, my sense of humour. A funny thing happened to me on my way to this island on the eve of this battle——

[*The crowd laugh. A familiar voice rings out.*]

BRANWEN: Olwen! Look here, girl! Muldoon!

OLWEN: The young man who ran away from us.

BRANWEN: Though he's not such a young man now.

OLWEN: But we look the same, don't we?

MULDOON: Except for your lack of faces.

OLWEN: Oh, don't you think figures more important?

BRANWEN: Never mind faces or figures, we've both got new jobs, we're happy.

OLWEN: And I've got more than a job. I've got a nice little cottage.

MULDOON: With bells on the bed?

OLWEN: Bells, Muldoon bach? A whole symphony!

BRANWEN: But listen to me; *I* have a bower of birch trees with honeysuckle and hot and cold water——

[*Another familiar voice intrudes.*]

MILLER: Is it Muldoon? the name's Miller.

MULDOON: Ah, the Miller of Hell.

MILLER: Certainly not. I am a promoter. How can I promote you?

MULDOON: You can help me to find the Lord of the Eskers.

MILLER: Still on the old tack? If you take *my* advice——

INVENTOR: Muldoon! You missed an experience.

MULDOON: Who're you? Oh, of course, the alchemist.

INVENTOR: Excuse me: nuclear scientist.

MULDOON: I thought you had blown yourself up.

INVENTOR: Me? But I'm a dreamer; I only blow up other people. Which reminds me: I'm looking for a passage to the mainland.

MULDOON: I'm not going to the mainland.

INVENTOR: But that's where he is, you know.

MULDOON: He? Who?

INVENTOR: The person you're looking for. Though why you've got to use a knife when you could do it by remote control——

QUEEN: You! I knew I should find you again!

The Mad Islands

MULDOON: The Queen of the Twilight! I thought you
were killed by the sun.

QUEEN: I thought so too. I fainted. When I recovered
I was out in the open under the blazing blue
bowl of the sky and the flowers were all
open and the birds all singing and at once I
thought of you—because it was you who
gave me this.

MULDOON: Why are you the only one here with a face?
Not but what the face has changed.

QUEEN: Of course it has. I am now Queen of the
Morning.

[*A seal barks in the distance.*]

QUEEN: Was that a seal? It sounded like a seal.

INVENTOR: It couldn't be a seal. It came from the liner.

[*The seal barks again.*]

QUEEN: It does come from the liner.

INVENTOR: Excuse me, madam, I speak as a scientist.
Seals are not found on liners.

[*The seal barks a third time.*]

QUEEN: Well, in that case, it's not a seal—but,
whatever it is, it's my enemy.

SKERRIE [*off*]: Muldoon! Come back! Before it's too late!
Gather your men and come back on board!

CORMAC: Muldoon, Muldoon, I've been looking for
you everywhere. I have a singing in my ears.
I had it once before—on the eve of a battle.

QUEEN: A battle, did you say? I can prevent your
battles. Where are my handmaids? Branwen!
Olwen!

BRANWEN:
OLWEN: }Here, lady.

QUEEN: Have you the baskets with the doves of peace
in them?

BRANWEN: I have the white doves.

OLWEN: I have the black doves.

QUEEN: Good. Now stand back all of you. I will have

no fighting on this island. Branwen! Olwen!
Let loose the doves of peace!

[*There is a whirring of pigeons rising and then a cooing and whirring mixed.*]

MILLER: Very well promoted! More grist to my mill!

CORMAC: Up the white doves! The whites for ever!
Down with the black doves! Down with them!

URSACH: Down with your white doves, Cormac!
And down with you too, damn you!

[MULDOON'S *crew divide into two parties to fight each other to the death.*]

CROWD: Up the Whites! The Whites!
Up the Blacks! The Blacks!

MULDOON: Stop fightingl Cormac! Ursach! Fiosta,
Brian, all of you! Stop fighting! Put up your
swords!

CORMAC: Swords? Give me my sten!

[*There is a burst from a sten gun and then mixed machine-gun fire, grenades, etc.; then silence except for odd groanings.*]

QUEEN: I didn't mean this to happen.

MULDOON: Queen of the Morning? You are still Queen
of the Twilight. As for your doves of
peace——

URSACH: Muldoon! Muldoon! Come and listen before
I die.

MULDOON: Ursach! . . . Yes, Ursach?

URSACH: Listen, I have something to tell you . . .
about your mother . . . your mother and the
Lord of——

[*He gasps and can say no more.*]

MULDOON: Goodbye, Ursach. God have mercy on your
soul.

CORMAC: Is that Muldoon? Can't see for the blood in
my eyes.

MULDOON: Cormac! You're still alive!

CORMAC: No, I'm just going. We have all killed each
other. It is your move now, Muldoon.

The Mad Islands

MULDOON: Goodbye to you too, foster-brother.

INVENTOR: Excuse me, Muldoon, why not call it a day? I take it you're returning to the mainland now?

MULDOON: *Now* I might as well. I have lost every man of my crew.

JESTER: Always excepting me.

MULDOON: You! But I saw you fall!

JESTER: That was a stage fall.

SKERRIE [*calling*]: Come on board! Hurry! Hurry!

INVENTOR: Yes, hurry. The world won't wait for us.

[*They hurry. The* QUEEN *has the last word.*]

QUEEN: Branwen! Olwen! Call in the doves of peace!

[*The woodpigeons, still cooing, return to their mistress while* MULDOON *sails back to the port which he left so long ago. But this time he travels in a speedy modern liner.*]

INVENTOR: My dear fellow, do tell me more. You really mean that Muldoon is engaged in a kind of vendetta?

JESTER: He's been on it since—never mind when.

INVENTOR: But that sort of thing's so old-fashioned. Apart from being somewhat inhumane.

JESTER: What are *you* going to do when we get to the mainland?

INVENTOR: But I've told you already.

JESTER: You have. You're going straight to the municipal authorities to borrow their pneumatic drills. And then you're going to take up the world.

INVENTOR: Oh, not the whole world, I'm only going to drill through the crust. Just to prove that the earth is hollow. The municipal authorities have been very kind and enlightened.

JESTER: I always wondered why they called it the Port of the Unwise. How did you persuade them in the first place?

The Mad Islands

INVENTOR: Oh, I didn't have to persuade them. It was all arranged by a man called Miller——

[*The ship's siren sounds: they are approaching port.*]

JESTER: Well, would you believe it! We're practically there!

[*The siren sounds again. Farther along the deck* SKERRIE *is briefing* MULDOON.]

SKERRIE: When you go ashore now, Muldoon, just remember what I have been telling you. What you've got to do, do quickly. And above all, when you leave the castle, come straight back here to the quayside——

MULDOON: Where you'll be waiting for me.

SKERRIE: Where I'll be waiting for you. And what was the one other point?

MULDOON: I am not to go near the square. But you did not tell me why.

SKERRIE: Our friend over there will be using the square and only a fool and his road-drills will stay with him.

[*The siren sounds a third time and the noise dissolves into the noise of road-drills. This is the port and this is the square in it.*]

JESTER: I may be only a fool——

INVENTOR: Speak up, I can't hear you.

JESTER: I may be only a fool but I can't see the object of this.

INVENTOR: I've told you a dozen times: to prove that the earth is hollow.

JESTER: If it is, what will you do with it?

INVENTOR: It will aid my more general thesis that the centre of everything is nothing.

JESTER: Oh, I see. All nice and tidy.

INVENTOR: Your friend, Muldoon, when he gets to the castle, will probably prove something similar. But he's only one door to pass through; his test will be over sooner.

[MULDOON *is already waiting at this door.*]

62

The Mad Islands

PORTER: Now who is it you're wanting to see?

MULDOON: The Lord of the Eskers. Is he in?

PORTER: Of course he's in. What name will I say?

MULDOON: *I'll* say it.

PORTER: Muldoon?

MULDOON: You never heard of me?

PORTER: No, sir. Just wait here a moment, please.

[*Hollow steps receding—distant murmur—steps returning.*]

The Lord of the Eskers never heard of you either.

But don't be shy, go on in.

MULDOON: I won't be shy. Nor will this knife be shy.

[MULDOON *brushes off the porter and as he enters the castle, his steps ring hollow. When he reaches the central chamber he is met by a little boy.*]

I am Muldoon. I have come here at last to——

Where is the Lord of the Eskers?

BOY: You asked to see *me?*

MULDOON: You?

BOY: What do you want with me, old man?

MULDOON: I wanted vengeance but—where is the Lord of the Eskers?

BOY: I told you already. It's me.

[*Pause.*]

MULDOON: I see it now. How long have you held the title?

BOY: Two or three years. Since my father died.

MULDOON: I am too late then. He died.

BOY: If you had any request of him——

MULDOON: I had one request only—to kill him.

BOY: What! To kill him! Why?

MULDOON: It was he that killed my father.

BOY: I do not believe it.

MULDOON: It's true.

BOY: But when and where? He never killed anyone.

MULDOON: It was with this knife. In a church.

BOY: In a church? Oh, that was my grandfather.

MULDOON: And he's dead too?

BOY: No one knows. He abdicated long before I was born. He put himself to sea in a boat without oars for penance. He would be shockingly old now.

MULDOON: To sea . . . for penance? Did he come from Wales?

BOY: Of course not, he was the Lord of the Eskers. But he had been brought up in Wales and his wife, my grandmother, was Welsh. They say he was very unfaithful though.

MULDOON: I must go back then. To the island before the last. But I think I no longer need this.

BOY: Why are you offering me this knife?

MULDOON: It belongs to the Lord of the Eskers.

[*In accordance with* SKERRIE's *instructions* MULDOON *returns with all speed to the quay. But the* INVENTOR *is still busy in the square: his drills are about to break through.*]

INVENTOR: You can leave me, you know, if you're frightened.

JESTER: I'm frightened all right but I'll stay with you for the laugh.

Mother of God, there's Muldoon coming out of the castle. Well, he got the killing over quickly. Look at him now, he's breaking into a run.

INVENTOR: Why should I look at these figures of the past? When I've almost broken through to the future! If you *must* look at something, look at this!

[*The drills break through with an enormous noise. This noise continues and grows.*]

JESTER: And on the seventh day . . . he created nothing at all.

INVENTOR: Are you looking? The dust is thick but——

JESTER: I can see all I want to.

INVENTOR: I can't, I'm blinded with the dust. What can you see? Tell me!

JESTER: I can see nothing at all. Nothing, pure undiluted nothing. I mean: the whole thing's hollow.

INVENTOR: Hollow? Then I was right!

JESTER: You were indeed! *Dead* right!

[*Things begin to explode.*]

INVENTOR: Eureka! Eureka! It was worth it!

JESTER: The laugh is on me. I was dying . . . to get one.

[*The explosion reaches a climax just as* MULDOON *arrives on the quayside.*]

SKERRIE: Quick now! Into the boat! Before the tidal wave comes.

[*He jumps in. It is a motor boat.*]

Now then. Start up the engine!

[*The motor boat starts and they head once again for the open sea.*]

MULDOON: Look back. You can't see where it was.

SKERRIE: All the houses have gone down the hole. The Port of the Unwise has vanished.

MULDOON: The castle's gone too. The Lord of the Eskers is dead.

SKERRIE: Yet you still want to see his grandfather?

MULDOON: I don't want to see him but I must.

SKERRIE: Why?

MULDOON: I don't know.

SKERRIE: When you saw him before you still had the knife. But now, Muldoon——

MULDOON: Don't go on. This has all happened before. I know what you're going to say next. And I know, though I cannot face it, I know what's about to happen.

SKERRIE: That's the double vision of the mind. I know

it too, I'm afraid. In a moment we shall see the rock of the hermit, he will be standing there waiting——

MULDOON: And beside him a woman, old, very old, but still straight——

SKERRIE: And you know who she is?

MULDOON: No.

SKERRIE: I do.

[*The engine stalls.*]

MULDOON: Damn it, the engine's stalled. Wait now till I crank it——

[*He tries to crank it but fails.*]

What's wrong with it, I wonder.

[*A voice from the past calls out across the water.*]

MOTHER: Take your head out of that box! Look up! Raise your head, man, look at me!

MULDOON: Christ upon the naked tree! This has all happened before. The rock, the old hermit standing there, the woman beside him, waiting——

Woman! Old woman! Who *are* you?

MOTHER: I *was* a woman but now——Let the scales drop from your eyes.

[*They do but he cannot accept it.*]

MULDOON: No! No! No!

SKERRIE: Don't close your eyes, Muldoon. Look at her!

HERMIT: She is your mother—and she's dead.

MULDOON: And what has she to do with you?

HERMIT: Everything, my son, everything.

MULDOON: When you say 'my son' . . . do you speak as a man of God?

HERMIT: I speak as a man who once was a man of sin.

[*Pause.*]

MULDOON: Mother! Is that true?

MOTHER: I was his mistress. You are his son.

MULDOON: Then the man who was stabbed in the church——

HERMIT: It was I who stabbed him.

MOTHER: It was I who planned it. That man was my husband but not your father.

MULDOON: Then this quest of vengeance . . . ?

HERMIT: I had been unfaithful to her.

MOTHER: Yes, I wanted him killed. It was only the reason was different. But now we are back together and he is about to die.

HERMIT: Yes, Muldoon, my son, I am about to die. And may God have mercy on your soul.

MULDOON: On my soul! And yours?

HERMIT: Your mother and I will dissolve in foam; we shall have no souls between us.

MOTHER: Give me your hand, lost love of my life! Goodbye, Muldoon my son. Hand in hand your parents are now about to leave you.

MULDOON: I can't see this! I can't! I won't!

[*There is a double splash as the two bodies hit the sea.*]

SKERRIE: Open your eyes again. They have gone. They are foam already.

[*Pause.*]

MULDOON: Did you know, Skerrie?

SKERRIE: Who was your true father? I knew that only just now—just before I stalled your engine. And that changed everything else.

MULDOON: What else?

SKERRIE: I thought I could break the rules but you human beings are too difficult.

MULDOON: Let us go, Skerrie; I'll start up the engine again. We'll leave this deserted rock and——

SKERRIE: It is not deserted, not yet. Look up, Muldoon, see who's there!

MULDOON: Mother of God! Who is that naked man?

SKERRIE: He also has been waiting.

[*Yet another voice from the past calls out from the same rock.*]

DROWNED MAN: I have, Skerrie. For you.

MULDOON: What do you mean? Who are you?

DROWNED MAN: You met me before. Many years ago. Only you have grown older and I, Muldoon, have not.

SKERRIE: Yes, you have met him before. When you first saw him he was still one of you; under your eyes he became one of us.

DROWNED MAN: Will you come with me now, Skerrie?

SKERRIE: Not till you have answered three questions. When did you first meet the sea?

DROWNED MAN: In a singing shell and the music haunted me.

SKERRIE: Why did you become a seaman?

DROWNED MAN: Because I had heard of the joy of the sea.

SKERRIE: Thirdly and lastly: what *is* the sea?

DROWNED MAN: The first and the last thing, the cradle and grave of life, the mother and mistress of all of us.

And now—will you come with me?

SKERRIE: Yes, now I will come; you are one of my kind.

MULDOON: She will not; you will have to fight for her.

SKERRIE: Muldoon! Muldoon! Would you strike a drowned man?

MULDOON: A drowned man? Now I remember! But *that* man became a seal.

DROWNED MAN: And a seal I am. Look, here is my skin.

SKERRIE: Put it on, be quick, put it on! Then dive from that rock. I will join you.

MULDOON: Skerrie, you can't, you've been with me so long, without you I would be nowhere——

[*The* DROWNED MAN, *a seal again, dives from the rock.*]

You're right. He's a great grey seal.

SKERRIE: Give me your lips, Muldoon. Our first kiss and our last. I thought I could break the rules—I could have perhaps if you'd helped me.

The engine will work when I've gone.

The Mad Islands

Goodbye—and your strange God bless you.

[*She dives overboard and the splash ripples outwards.*]

MULDOON [*calling*]: Skerrie! Skerrie! . . . [*and then to himself*]
Two round heads swimming away.

[*calling again*] Goodbye then, Skerrie.

[*A seal barks.*]

MULDOON: So here am I at the end alone in a small boat
and it has all been for what? I thought that
vengeance was mine but the fates took it
away from me and what was I avenging anyway? My mother's name and shame—and
my father's—are lost for ever in foam, the
port from which I sailed is a gaping hole in
the globe, my foster brother and my friends
are dead, and Skerrie . . . Skerrie has left me.
Well, let's try once more. She said it should
work now.

[*He makes two vain attempts at cranking; at the third the
engine starts and the motorboat carries him away.*]

THE ADMINISTRATOR

Main Characters

JERRY, PROFESSOR OF PHYSICS
MARTHA, HIS WIFE
BILL BRYSON, A YOUNG LECTURER IN PHYSICS
THE DOCTOR, A GERMAN
ROBERT, ONCE MARTHA'S LOVER
EUNICE, AN AMERICAN JOURNALIST
CAPTAIN VORTREKKER, A WHITE HUNTER
LEPER BOY, AN AFRICAN BEATER
THE INTERIOR DECORATOR
A PROSECUTING COUNSEL
A PRIME MINISTER
A JUDGE
SALLY, MARTHA'S DAUGHTER

'The Administrator' was first broadcast in the B.B.C. Third Programme on 10 March 1961. Details are as follows:

Mrs King [Martha]	Mary Wimbush
Professor King [Jerry]	Russell Napier
Bill Bryson	Jon Rollason
The Doctor	David Hadda
Robert	Michael Turner
Eunice	Tucker McGuire
Leper Boy	Bloke Modisane
Sally	Sheila Grant
Prosecuting Council	Ralph Hallett

Other parts played by members of the B.B.C. Drama Repertory Company
Special Effects by the Radiophonic Workshop
Produced by Louis MacNeice

THE ADMINISTRATOR

A husband and wife are talking together in the evening.

MARTHA: So you're not going to take it, Jerry?

JERRY: No, darling.

MARTHA: It's the difference it would make, not only the money, the——

JERRY: If you want to keep up with the Joneses——

MARTHA: I want to get away from here. At least there'd be some green fields.

JERRY: And a beautiful chimney two hundred feet high.

MARTHA: Well, as there was at Harwell.

JERRY: Yes, so there was. I name this reactor Dinky.

MARTHA: But, Jerry, damn it, it's your subject. And for once you'd be your own boss.

JERRY: You think so? 'Your pass, sir! Where's your pass?' Director indeed! You know what the ghost of Achilles says in Homer? I'd rather be the most miserable drudge among the living than a king down here behind the security fence. Than a *King* down here among the twittering——

MARTHA: Trouble with you is——

JERRY: When I was a little boy, I *liked* being called King.

[*The telephone rings:* JERRY *answers it.*]

Yes, this is Professor King. Oh, Bill! . . . Yes, I was expecting you hours ago but it's not too late now, no, of course not.

MARTHA: It *is* too late.

JERRY: No, just you jump on your scooter and we'll talk about the Japanese fishermen.

[*He replaces the receiver.*]

MARTHA: Why do you indulge that very pushing young man?

JERRY: Because he's the future—and the future's got to be pushing.

MARTHA: That comes well from a man who's turning down the chance of a lifetime.

JERRY: Whose lifetime?

[*Pause.*]

MARTHA: If you don't give a damn for yourself, at least you've got two children.

JERRY: *You've* got two children.

MARTHA: That's mean of you.

JERRY: It's you that's always reminding me Sally is Robert's.

MARTHA: Yes, I'm mean too; I know it. But I'm not being mean when I ask you to take this job.

JERRY: 'Strictly peaceful purposes'. In the war plants that made saucepans started making machine guns.

MARTHA: Oh, you and your bomb!

JERRY: Yes, me and my bomb . . . Mine.

MARTHA: I just think you're escapist.

JERRY: Of course I'm escapist. Like an artist.

MARTHA: Research is research is research. But, whatever you say, it's not like painting a picture. You can hide your head in the pure, pure sand but, whatever you dig up there, those other people can use it.

JERRY: You're absolutely right, of course.

MARTHA: Then why not take a job where——

JERRY: Where I'd be my own boss? I'd not be! As Director of that bloody Institute, you know what I'd be? I'd——

[*The door bell rings.*]

MARTHA: *He* was quick. Must have rung from the box round the corner. I suppose he'll keep you up for hours again telling you his piddling little grievances.

JERRY: Well, you go to bed, darling.

[*She goes upstairs and her place is taken by a brash young man.*]

MARTHA: Yes, exit the Red Brick Wife. But, if Bill

Bryson starts shouting and wakes up the children again——

BILL: You know, Kingpin . . .

JERRY: What, Bill?

BILL: I don't think your wife likes me. Oh, I don't blame her, she couldn't with her background.

JERRY: It's the same as mine.

BILL: She's not a physicist. Piles may be an almost universal affliction but not the kind you and I suffer from, eh?

JERRY: You're wrong; our kind's only too universal. Anyhow your sense of humour's crude, Bill. Now this piece of yours on the Japanese fishermen—— You'll get your Doctorate all right, you know.

BILL: I know. What I don't know is what I'll do after it. Except that I won't stay here. In this dump? Not on your life! It may be too late for *you* to get out of it——

JERRY: You'd be surprised.

BILL: What at?

JERRY: Got a threepenny stamp on you?

BILL: No.

JERRY: That's all that lies between me and a great refusal.

BILL: Great refusal of what?

JERRY: It's hush-hush; only my wife knows.

BILL: Job back at Harwell?

JERRY: I'm not allowed to tell you.

BILL: Anyhow you're refusing it?

JERRY: Yes.

BILL: And what does Mrs King think?

JERRY: She's seen photographs of the house we'd have. Interiors taken with a wide-angled lens. Also there's a lot of prestige attached.

BILL: And money?

JERRY: Oh, a packet.

BILL: And power?

JERRY: Up to a point. Shall we say 'and influence'?

BILL: Hm. If I were you I'd take it like a bloody flash.

JERRY: But you don't know what it is.

BILL: Money and power—that's good enough for me. I agree with the Bard, you know: there is a tide in the affairs, etcetera.

JERRY: But it didn't lead on to fortune. 'The strings, my lord, are false.' Brutus lost that battle.

BILL: You know, Professor King, I think you're a dreamer.

JERRY: You're wrong, Bill, it's the hardheads like you are dreamers; you dream of becoming tycoons as if this were fifty years ago. And Cabinet Ministers dream of remaining Cabinet Ministers. And my wife of course is a dreamer; she dreams she can put the clock back or jump on the needle on the record or keep the eggs soft-boiled by turning the egg-boiler round or . . .

[*His voice fades away and we join* MARTHA, *who is dreaming at this moment. She is giving a large party. They are all talking about success.*]

MARTHA: Oh, Lady Jones! Do come into my dream! I expect you know everyone here, so first of all what about a drink? Champagne or something else?

LADY JONES: Champagne, please. This is your house-warming, isn't it, Mrs King?

MARTHA: Yes. It's the first we've ever had in fact. But then, my husband was never a Director before.

LADY JONES: Well, you've got a lovely house to warm, my dear. Especially this room: so light and bright and such a good view of the Institute.

The Administrator

MARTHA: We get the same view from our bedroom.
Jerry wanted to sleep at the back but . . .

LADY JONES: You got your own way? I expect you always do.

MARTHA: Not always. I had my work cut out getting
him to come here at all. I only swung him at
the eleventh hour. He'd had a terrible young
man to see him that evening. A real nasty
little climber; he put cigarette ash everywhere.

[*From* MARTHA'*s dream we return to the wide-awake world
of the sitting room.*]

JERRY: No, just drop it on the floor, Bill. To return
to Aldermaston, you really can't understand?

BILL: No, I can't. But I also can't understand this:
if you feel like that, why don't you go
marching too?

JERRY: Hardly possible in my position.

BILL: I thought you didn't mind about position.

JERRY: The big brothers peer at me enough as it is.
Besides I hate demonstrations.

BILL: Still, you believe they're right, the uni-
lateralist boys?

JERRY: They're the only ones who're not wrong.

BILL: God almighty!

JERRY: Keep your voice down, Bill. The children.

BILL: Who was that old Greek wallah who rolled
the stone up the hill? And it always rolled
bloody well down again.

JERRY: Sisyphus.

BILL: That's right: Sisyphus. Well, that stone was
how much in circumference? Not twenty-
five thousand miles, eh? Right. Even if old
Sisyphus had worn a duffle coat and had had
that Canon of St Paul's putting his shoulder
to it too—well, I ask you, speaking globally
—talk about being a dreamer!

79

JERRY: Talk about being a dreamer, I asked you to keep your voice down. The children are supposed to be sleeping. And I dare say my wife is too.

BILL: And what will they all be dreaming of?

JERRY: Well, Sally might be dreaming of a new long-playing record——

BILL: Cool?

JERRY: Cool. Or maybe a new pair of jeans. And Thomas might be dreaming of a brand-new air-gun. Or a joke fried egg or a space suit. My family, I must tell you, simply love getting presents.

BILL: Better if they get 'em in dreams then. No trouble for *you*, Kingpin.

[*On this cue we are back at* MARTHA's *party.*]

MARTHA: Oh, Robert, what marvellous roses! Robert, have you met Lady Jones? Lady Jones, this is a very old friend of mine; we knew each other at Cambridge——

LADY JONES: You were undergraduates together?

MARTHA: No, we were just together. I was the Provost's daughter. And he brought me roses even then. But why are these ones so blown, Robert?

[*Pause.*]

Why are these roses so blown?

LADY JONES: But they're not, Mrs King, they're just buds.

MARTHA: Lise! Lise!

LISE: Yes, please?

MARTHA: Bring a dustpan and brush at once. I won't have these petals on the carpet!
Robert, you've let me down.

[*Pause.*]

Why have you let me down?

[*Pause.*]

80

The Administrator

Robert, can't you hear what I say?
[*Pause.*]

LADY JONES: He's gone, Mrs King.

MARTHA: Gone!

[*The bedroom door opens, startling* MARTHA *and waking her.*]
Robert!

JERRY: Sorry, darling, did I wake you? In that case I'll put the light on.

[*He does so.*]

MARTHA: No, don't, don't—my eyes. Sorry, I was dreaming. Has Bill Bryson gone?

JERRY: Yes, just. Good old Bill, he thinks I'm too starry-eyed.

MARTHA: And for once he's right. Jerry?

JERRY: Yes?

MARTHA: You won't reconsider it? The Institute? They're handing it to you on a plate.

JERRY: And when he looked at it again he saw it was his own head.

MARTHA: What are you talking about?

JERRY: Which would make you Salome and as for King Herod—no, of course I can't take the damned job.

MARTHA: Can't? Won't, you mean.

JERRY: Won't, then. Sorry, darling, but I'm just not an administrator.

MARTHA: I think you've got no guts. I also think you're very selfish.

[*Pause.*]

There are the children after all.

JERRY: Sally . . . Thomas . . . yes.

MARTHA: You've no right to pass up this chance for them. Or perhaps you have for Thomas—with him, I suppose, we each have an equal say——

JERRY: But with Sally the say is all yours?

MARTHA: I know what Robert would want.

JERRY: A curious logic. Because I have to bring up another man's child you expect me to alter my whole way of life, to take on something I hate, to——

MARTHA: Who was driving the car?

JERRY: Won't you ever drop that? Look, darling, go to sleep.

MARTHA: Have you written to the Institute?

JERRY: Yes.

MARTHA: Posted it?

JERRY: No.

MARTHA: In that case——

JERRY: You say you know what Robert would want. Well, I knew him as well as you did——

MARTHA: You did not! And I remember him saying, as between the child and the parent, the child should always come first.

JERRY: And so he thought nothing of fathering illegits.

MARTHA: That's cheap. You know very well he was waiting for a divorce.

JERRY: Sorry. She'd never have given him one, of course.

MARTHA: How you know all the answers! But don't let's go round that dismal treadmill again, let's get back to the Institute——

JERRY: You seriously think you want it for the children?

MARTHA: I want it for all of us. I suppose in the last analysis everyone puts himself first but . . .

JERRY: But what?

MARTHA: But nothing. Do this for me, Jerry.

[*Pause.*]

I don't often ask you to do things for me.

JERRY: No, but when you do . . . Though perhaps that time it was Sally did the asking. Three months before she was born. Asked for a

home, for a name . . . Sally King . . . King.
As you say, I was driving the car.

MARTHA: I dreamt about Robert just now. He gave
me roses. They were blown.

[*Smothered sob and pause.*]

JERRY: Darling.

MARTHA: Yes?

JERRY: I shall sleep on it.

MARTHA: On what?

JERRY: On the decision.

MARTHA: I thought you *had* decided.

JERRY: So did I.
I'd better ask the telephone to call me.

[*This he does.*]

Hullo! This is Rampart 6945. Could you call
me, please, at seven-thirty to-morrow?
That's right; seven-thirty in the morning.

[*He replaces the receiver.*]

MARTHA: Jerry!

JERRY: 'm?

MARTHA: I know you think I'm a bitch, but before you
sleep on the decision . . . well . . . I don't
know how to put it, I know you think I'm a
bitch, but——

JERRY: Stop saying that, you silly.

MARTHA: I just want to tell you: whatever you decide
I'll accept. And I promise not to nag about it.

JERRY: Thank you, darling.

MARTHA: Thank *you*, Jerry.

JERRY: Now don't go having any more dreams——

MARTHA: Don't you either. Who was having dreams
last night that made him talk in his sleep!

JERRY: That was just my old recurrent.

MARTHA: The one at the top of the stairs? In the house
where you were a child. With all the old
trunks on the landing.

JERRY: Yes, but the point is the door. There was no

door there really, as I told you, and there never could have been a door because it's an outer wall. So naturally, whenever I see it there, I'm puzzled. And I stand there and stare at it and very slowly it opens. [*His voice is now very sleepy.*] It always creaks when it opens—I've told you how it always creaks— and then . . . well then, I never know . . .

[*Now he is asleep and a door creaks open to let him in.*]

DOCTOR [*German accent*]: Professor King?

JERRY: That's me.

DOCTOR: I am expecting you before this. Come through the door, please.

[*The door creaks shut.*]

DOCTOR: There. Now we are cosy. But you ask why I am expecting you. I will tell you: it is for business I am a doctor, you must understand. But first have a Japanese cigar—No, no, it is not radio-active. Now I have here one form to sign and then there will be the finger-prints. In case you do not come back.

JERRY: Excuse me, Doctor, that fish on the wall——

DOCTOR: I caught him myself; he was troubling the bathers.

But here is the pen. Sign, please.

Thank you.

And now the fingers.

Thank you.

Also the left hand.

Thank you.

Good. Now must we go. It is not for me to be late since I myself must unveil it. There will be brass bands, you understand. And all the ladies in their minks.

[*A brass band blossoms around them blowsily.*]

Your Excellencies, ladies and gentlemen! Before I unveil this statue of your late King,

The Administrator

I must remind you all for what this so great man stood. I myself have had often the privilege to meet him and not only to meet him but to extract his appendix; also his tonsils and one small cyst in his groin. Moreover I do on him prefrontal lobectomy. Hence can I tell you how great has he been. And not only great but he had such sense of fun. One time we are walking, your late King and I, along Kriegstrasse—it is in the spring—and as we are turning into Scheiss-strasse it is in the spring and we meet the Minister of Health. 'Good morning, Herr Minister', says your late King. 'Good morning, Your Majesty', says the Minister of Health. 'Ha!' says your late King, 'Now must we have a little fun, Herr Minister. Open the mouth and shut the eyes, please. That is right, Herr Minister, thank you; now please make protrude the tongue.' So what can he do, our poor Minister, he makes protrude the tongue but I can see he is trembling; it is in the spring and blows a cold wind down Scheiss-strasse. 'Ach Herr Minister!' cries your late King, 'What a bad and dirty tongue you have! How should you be Minister of Health when you have a tongue like that? Today must I have your resignation.' So the Minister resigns and no one hears of him since. But what makes this so funny, his tongue is clean all the time.

[*The dream crowd laugh loudly.*]

But now to more serious matters. The two great aims of your late King have been peace on earth and victory over his enemies. Also was he no mean amateur architect. Has he not designed our world-famous cenotaph!

You remember when he unveiled it? As
our national flag fell away from that great
aluminium cylinder came forth a gasp of
admiration. And next an outburst of sobbing.
Even so let it be today. Achtung! The
moment of truth. I take now this rope in my
hand and—Ein! Zwei!! Drei!!!

[*He unveils the appalling monument.*]

Behold! Your late King!

[*The crowd first gasp, then sob. Their sobbing fades into the distance.*]

A LOW VOICE [*in Jerry's ear*]:
Is it not brave to be a King, Techelles?
Usumcasane and Theridamas,
Is it not passing brave to be a King——

JERRY [*shouting, still in his dream*]: And ride in
triumph——

MARTHA: Jerry!

JERRY [*waking*]: What?

MARTHA: Stop it!

JERRY: Stop what?

MARTHA: Talking in your sleep.

JERRY: Was I?

MARTHA: In fact you were shouting. Have a glass of
water; you feel all sweaty.

JERRY: No, thank you.

MARTHA: Now we're both awake I'd like to talk to you.

JERRY: I said I'd sleep on it, didn't I?

MARTHA: You didn't say you'd shout on it. Oh, I know
you think I'm a bitch but——

JERRY: Darling, it's time you got a new theme song.
I don't think you're a bitch. I do think
you're difficult.

MARTHA: Who's not among the people we know? At
least among the wives we know.

JERRY: Maybe scientists ought to be monks.

MARTHA: You've got something there, Jerry.

JERRY: And yet my old man was a sheep-farmer.
MARTHA: What's that got to do with it?
JERRY: *He* should have been a monk.
[*Pause.*]   If Robert were alive now, I wonder what
        he'd be doing.
MARTHA: He'd be married to me.
JERRY: I mean professionally.
MARTHA: I suppose he'd be some sort of high-up
        executive.
JERRY: Yes, I suppose he would.
        [*hums*] There is an Institute
                Far, far away . . .
        Sometimes one has to choose between being
        selfish and being dishonest.
MARTHA: Darling.
JERRY: Yes?
MARTHA: I'm not asking you to be dishonest. But I
        genuinely can't see how the Institute would
        conflict with——
JERRY: I know you genuinely can't. I think I *will*
        have a glass of water.
MARTHA: Just a moment then.
[*She turns on the light.*]
        You haven't got a fever, have you?
JERRY: No. Why?
[*She pours out a glass of water.*]
MARTHA: *My* dream didn't make me sweat.
JERRY: So you were dreaming too?
MARTHA: You interrupted it. Here.
[*She hands him the glass and he empties.*]
        [*sleepily*] Oh, I dare say I'll pick it up again,
        it's only like dropping a stitch in a pattern.
        Just unravel back the way poor Sally always
        has to—it might be even two or three rows,
        but once you get back to the point where you
        dropped it . . .
[*She is off again.*]   87

ROBERT: Well, well, Sally! That was a clanger, wasn't it?

MARTHA: It's not Sally, Robert, it's Martha.

ROBERT: Who's Sally then?

MARTHA: Your daughter.

ROBERT: Didn't know I had one.

MARTHA: You knew I was pregnant.

ROBERT: It might have been a son.

MARTHA: Would you have preferred a son?

ROBERT: I don't really know. Has she got a hooky nose like me?

MARTHA: No, she's not, thank God; she's got a feminine nose. Besides that would be hard on Jerry. People talked as it was.

ROBERT: It was very nice of Jerry to marry you.

MARTHA: It gave him a chance he'd always wanted.

ROBERT: That's ungenerous, my love.

MARTHA: He *was* driving the car.

ROBERT: He didn't have the smash on purpose.

MARTHA: No, of course he didn't, a skid is a skid. All the same, Robert——

ROBERT: It's usually the driver who buys it. The steering wheel smashes the sternum and——

MARTHA: We've had this conversation before.

ROBERT: Well, nothing's happened since—for me. Did you see me after it?

MARTHA: You know I did.

ROBERT: I don't. I was unconscious.

MARTHA: So was I—nearly. But Sally wasn't, she kept jumping.

ROBERT: Do they jump three months before birth?

MARTHA: Sally's the Olympic type. I do wish Jerry cared more about sport. That's another reason I want us to move; Sally needs more open air. It was all right when we were at Harwell but in this bloody city—all smog and television aerials—well, they do have

playing fields and she could belong to some
club but . . . No, the only person who could
ever get Jerry to take exercise was an awful
American bitch he used to take out in a punt.
She came to Cambridge for May Week——

ROBERT: You don't mean Eunice by any chance?

MARTHA: Don't tell me you knew her too!

ROBERT: You say that every time, darling.

MARTHA: Yes, and you always say 'I can't say I knew
her, I——'

ROBERT: '. . . just met her'.

MARTHA: That's right.

ROBERT: 'And it was years ago anyway.'

MARTHA: That's right.

ROBERT: And you never believe me.

MARTHA: That's right. And, since you are dead, nothing can ever be known.

[*A familiar door creaks open.*]

EUNICE: Walk right in, stranger! Long time no see.
'Will you walk into my jungle
Said the tarantula to the——'

JERRY: Eunice!

EUNICE: Hiya, old timer! Where did you get those
bags under your eyes?

JERRY: Where did you get that ravishing leopard-
skin coat?

EUNICE: I shot that ravishing leopard. I've gotten me
a column of my own now, Jerry. Syndicated
throughout all the fifty States. Bet you can't
guess my *nom de plume*?

JERRY: Tell me.

EUNICE: The Queen of Safari. And I've certainly
earned it, brother. See this handbag? I shot
that sucker too. *And* these shoes. Gee, the
jungle's great.

JERRY: I never even knew you could shoot.

EUNICE: I couldn't in your day; I learnt it from Ernest.

The Administrator

JERRY: Ernest?

EUNICE: *That* Ernest. Now don't be jealous, honey; Ernest's a sucking lamb. Besides, when he's not popping off with his 505 Greenhill, he's too goldarn busy with his ff fortissimo typewriter. Where's *your* 505 by the way? You'll need it where we're going.

JERRY: Oh, I never shoot with one of those.

EUNICE: What *is* your weapon then, sweetie-pie?

JERRY: Uranium 285.

EUNICE: Oh. Sure that's all right for the jungle?

JERRY: Yes, it's all right for the jungle.

EUNICE: Well, kiss me like you used to and we'll go.

[*Kiss.*]

It is like you used to, too. Will you never learn how to kiss, honey? Now, when your friend Robert took me out on the river——

JERRY: Robert's dead.

EUNICE: Is that so? I'm sorry; he was cute. Well, we've not much time before I go to press. Just hold your breath and jump when I tell you. Ready? One! Two! Three! Jump!

[*A macaw, or something, screams, and they are in a sizzling jungle.*]

Duck!

Jump again!

Duck again!

There!

Yeah, those liana creepers—they'd strangle you soon as look at you.

VORTREKKER [*Afrikaans accent*]: Eunice! Welcome back!

EUNICE: Why, it's Hennie! Hennie, this is Jerry King. Jerry, this is Captain Hennie Vortrekker. A white hunter if ever I met one.

VORTREKKER: A white hunter, ja; you ought to see my medals, man.

EUNICE: And his etchings.

The Administrator

VORTREKKER: Ja, and my etchings. You in a hurry for your column, Eunice?

EUNICE: Say, don't you know me by this time!

[*Through the noise of the jungle one can just hear the noise of typewriters.*]

How's the bloody spoor today?

VORTREKKER: Bloody. He's dying in there in the mangrove swamp.

EUNICE: Dying already? You might have told me!

VORTREKKER: If you're in a hurry, Eunice, you just go right in and finish him.

EUNICE: In these heels? Why not send in a beater?

VORTREKKER: Where's that beater?

LEPER BOY: Here, Bwana.

VORTREKKER: Ah, Leper Boy! Now you listenum. See that swamp where elephant grass go chuff-chuff? Mighty big beef for down there. O.K. Leper Boy go for down in swamp, beatum for beef, driveum for out.

LEPER BOY: What kindum beef, Bwana?

VORTREKKER: What kindum beef no matterum, Leper Boy. Memsahib wantum killum bang-bang.

EUNICE: Memsahib wantum killum columnwise.

LEPER BOY: O.K., Bwana. Leper Boy fetchum.

[*He splashes away into the gurgling swamp.*]

JERRY: Captain Vortrekker?

VORTREKKER: What?

JERRY: That beater of yours is crippled.

VORTREKKER: His not to reason why. Stand by to fire, Eunice.

JERRY [*to self*]: Eena—meena—mina—mo!
Catch a leper by his toe!

[*From the depth of the swamp comes the roar of a nightmare lion.*]

If he squeals——

LEPER BOY [*off*]: Helpum! Helpum! Old man lion!

[*EUNICE fires.*]

EUNICE: Got him! Plumb in the neck!

VORTREKKER: Too bad, Eunice. That's Leper Boy's neck.
[*The typewriters now re-emerge and conquer the jungle noises. They rattle out their copy and are silent.*]

MARTHA [*in her dream*]: And another thing, Robert; since you're dead, you can't answer me back. Just try and see what happens. Go on, Robert; don't stand there like a tailor's dummy with the roses melting away in your hands. I suppose you meant them for Eunice; explain that away if you can. But you can't explain anything away, you've got no mouth to explain with. Let alone a mind, let alone a mind, that's where Jerry has the edge on you. He's not what you would have been but at least he has a mouth and a mind. He's alive, you see, that's the point. You are, aren't you, Jerry?

[*The two dreams now begin to jostle.*]

JERRY: What's that?

MARTHA: I'm asking you: are you alive?

JERRY: Is who alive?

MARTHA: You.

JERRY: Leper Boy's not.

MARTHA: Don't care about him.

JERRY: It might start a chain reaction. Chain reaction . . . chain of office . . . Queen of Safari . . . King of Beasts . . . And away he went with his tufted tail and we followed the spoor through fifty states. There were mushrooms too . . . in the sky when we die . . .

MARTHA [*alarmed and about to wake*]: Jerry! Where have you gone?

JERRY: Nowhere.

MARTHA: Can't find you.

JERRY: Ow! Don't pinch.

MARTHA: So you *are*!

JERRY: What?

MARTHA: Alive. Sorry. I was dreaming.

The Administrator

JERRY: Were we talking to each other?

MARTHA: Yes. But I must just see if . . .

[*She turns on the light again.*]

MARTHA: No, hell, it's our same old room.

JERRY: Where did you think we were?

MARTHA: Oh, *you* weren't. There was concealed lighting. And a pink-tinted mirror by the bed. It was a dream room. Perhaps it's our room in the Director's House.

JERRY: Does it look out on a very high fence?

[*The sudden cry of a child comes from another room.*]

SALLY: Mummy! Mummy!

JERRY: Sally again.

MARTHA: Yes, Sally *again*! Why that child's always having nightmares I—— Now where the hell are my slippers?

JERRY [*sleepily*]: Come back soon.

MARTHA: Of course I will.

[*As she goes out, the bedroom door becomes the old creaking dream door. Beyond it is a pansy young man.*]

INTERIOR

DECORATOR: Excuse me. Are you the Director?

JERRY: Of course not.

INT. DEC.: But you must be, my dear. This is the Directorate. And this, I'm afraid, is my teeny-weeny bill.

JERRY: Bill! 'Graphite and polythene fitments a hundred and eighty pounds ten. Concealed lighting two hundred. Pink-tinted bedside mirror, seven foot by five, a hundred and fifty. Decontaminating apparatus——' Who authorized all this rubbish?

INT. DEC.: You did, my dear. You even specified the built-in aquariumette for the Javanese fighting fish. Personally I can't bear to look at them. Spiteful little things—they remind me so much of my prep. school.

The Administrator

JERRY: I'm not going to pay this bill.

INT. DEC.: Now don't be naughty, I beg you. I may be only a poor old interior decorator but I do have a heart just like everybody else. And tear-ducts, my dear, and tear-ducts.

JERRY: I tell you I'm not——

INT. DEC.: And of course a flair for design. You know I designed the security fence? Well, it's not very easy to make that sort of thing chic, but I think my success is proved by that poor little boy. You know, the one that got electrocuted. He wanted to climb it, I'm told, because he thought it so pretty. Like something out of a fairy story—one of those impregnable castles. However, one's just got to lump it; security, my dear, is security. To return to my tiddily-widdily bill——

JERRY: I'm not going to pay it, I tell you.

[MARTHA *returns, awake, to cut in on her husband's dream.*]

MARTHA: Sally's all right. Not such a bad nightmare as hers go.

JERRY: A nightmare! What do you call that mirror?

MARTHA: What mirror?

JERRY: I'm not that colour and I never want to be.

MARTHA: Stop dreaming, Jerry!

JERRY [*waking*]: Eh?

MARTHA: There's no future in it.

JERRY: That's just what I'm afraid there is.

MARTHA: What were you dreaming about?

JERRY: I think I took over where you left off. Could be an omen. That bill is exorbitant.

MARTHA: You're still not properly awake.

JERRY: Was there an aquarium in the room?

MARTHA: What room?

JERRY: The room you were dreaming about?

MARTHA: An aquarium? Of course not. There were a couple of budgies.

94

JERRY: Fighting each other?

MARTHA: Far from it.

JERRY: Then it's not the same room. What was Sally dreaming about?

MARTHA: She was in some very modern submarine that had got stuck on the bottom.

JERRY: That will serve. Poor Sally.

My usual—the creaking door—I've had it twice tonight.

MARTHA: That's more than your ration; once per night is enough. I know you think I'm a bitch, darling, but I do worry about you. So promise me: no more tonight. Promise?

[*Lingering on this dubious word* JERRY *falls asleep.*]

JERRY: Promise . . . Promise . . . Promise . . .

1ST QUIZ VOICE: Seven-letter word going down.

ELEVATOR BOY: Going down!

[*A lift descends, taking* JERRY *into a deeper dream.*]

1ST QUIZ VOICE: As a young man showed exceptional.

2ND QUIZ VOICE: His early was never fulfilled.

3RD QUIZ VOICE: He made a solemn to his wife.

JERRY: I didn't, did I?

1ST QUIZ VOICE: Of better things but things got worse.

2ND QUIZ VOICE: Of a fine day but it clouded over.

3RD QUIZ VOICE: Of a new era but new in what?

ALL: Solemn. Exceptional. Never fulfilled.

[*The dream door creaks again, opening.*]

USHER: Come in.

[*The door closes:* JERRY *has entered the law-courts. People appear to be expecting him.*]

Silence in the Court!

[*Silence.*]

CLERK OF THE COURT: Members of the Jury, the Prisoner at the Bar, Professor Jeremiah King, is charged that contrary to the interest of himself and his family he did on the seventeenth inst. commit an act of self-deception, to wit——

The Administrator

AN OWL [*it would appear*]: Tu-whoo! A cheerful note
While Jerry King doth turn his coat.
Tu-whit! Tu-whoo! [*etc.*]

[*Laughter.*]

JUDGE: Remove that owl. And if there is any more laughter I shall have the Court cleared. This is a temple of justice—not a ruined abbey or an aviary. Proceed, Mr Carpingdale.

PROSECUTING COUNSEL: Members of the Jury, I will not beat about the ivy-tod. The Prisoner at the Bar, I am told, is known among his pupils as the King-pin. This nickname I shall prove is ironic. Jeremiah King is nothing more than a small and somewhat faulty cog in a vast and complex machine. But when he had a chance to become a much bigger cog, to become a highly paid administrator instead of a mere teacher and research worker, what did he do? He wilfully forewent this chance on the grounds that he was more use where he was, that he was unsuited to the higher post and that, if he took this higher post, he might be exploited by the State or have to endorse decisions of which he did not personally approve. I put it to you, Members of the Jury, that in thus refusing to take the tide at the flood he was actuated by nothing higher or deeper than timidity, indolence and self-ishness. It appears in fact that he has always been anti-Establishment——

JUDGE: Will you kindly explain that phrase.

PROS. COUNSEL: I mean, my lord, that he has always been opposed to the Establishment.

JUDGE: And what exactly is the Establishment?

PROS. COUNSEL: The top people, my lord. The people who can run the show by just walking it. The people who keep in by sitting it out. The noble company of Gadarenes who run not down hill but up. The people whom Disraeli described as——

JUDGE: Do they wear wigs?

PROS. COUNSEL: Some of them, my lord.

JUDGE: I see. Continue.

PROS. COUNSEL: This man King, being opposed to the Establishment, is like those politicians who from years of being in opposition have lost all desire to be in office. Such a man, as we all well know, if his party did get into power, would find himself acutely embarrassed.

[*The creaking door opens again, taking* JERRY *from the court to the Cabinet.*]

PRIME MINISTER: King, my dear fellow! Come in and join us. Why are you hanging about out there in the lobby? It's warmer in here in the Cabinet and we've just had our foam rubber cushions installed. Just cross the threshold, it's only a step. Come on, man, shake your stumps; just come across and——

1ST QUIZ VOICE: Three-letter word across.

2ND QUIZ VOICE: It is an awkward. Take a niblick to it.

3RD QUIZ VOICE: You must forgive him. It's only a white.

1ST QUIZ VOICE: It's a black and unforgivable.

2ND QUIZ VOICE: He intended a truth but it turned to a——

[*The door shuts as* JERRY *commits himself inside.*]

PRIME MINISTER: Good man, you've made it! Take a pew, take a drink, take a cake-mix. Nice office this, isn't it?

JERRY: Yes, Prime Minister, but before I join your Cabinet——

PRIME MINISTER: What do you mean? You *have* joined it! Don't look so worried, man. This Cabinet's mine, not Dr Caligari's. What are you staring at, King?

JERRY: That mirror.

The Administrator

PRIME MINISTER: What about it? We got it on the Never Never.

JERRY: But we all look so healthy in it.

VOICES: Hear, Hear!

JERRY: So young and bonny and pink and——

PRIME MINISTER: Yes, don't we. I had it tinted.

JERRY: But it's not us!

1ST QUIZ VOICE: Before acquiring office they had dropped many an assuring.

2ND QUIZ VOICE: They had dropped many words of honeyed.

3RD QUIZ VOICE: But whatever they dropped they——

[*A trayful of crockery somewhere falls with a horrible crash.*]

1ST QUIZ VOICE: Seven-letter word going down.

[*The lift whizzes down and back and* JERRY *is back in the law-court.*]

ROBERT: I swear by Almighty God that I shall tell the truth, the whole truth and nothing but the truth.

PROS. COUNSEL: Your name is Robert Leeson, erstwhile friend of the Prisoner's?

ROBERT: Yes.

PROS. COUNSEL: You were, by profession, an administrator?

ROBERT: Yes.

PROS. COUNSEL: What did you administrate?

ROBERT: Anything that came along. If I had the chance now, I think I would go for television. Unless it was public relations.

PROS. COUNSEL: Kindly confine yourself to what you knew in your lifetime. When you were a friend of the Prisoner's could he also have been described as an administrator?

ROBERT: I don't think so. He had a blind spot for some things.

PROS. COUNSEL: What did he not have blind spots for?

ROBERT: Well, er . . . creative work, I suppose.

PROS. COUNSEL: What work?

[*Laughter in court.*]

Will you kindly repeat that phrase.

The Administrator

ROBERT: I said creative work.

PROS. COUNSEL: 'Work'? Being an administrator yourself, you would still admit that such people—these so-called creative types—do work of a sort?

ROBERT: Certainly.

PROS. COUNSEL: What is the difference between the two types? Between you, for instance, and the Prisoner.

ROBERT: Well, um . . . the administrator manages other people. The creative types get on with things on their own.

PROS. COUNSEL: In other words the creative types are more selfish?

ROBERT: I didn't mean that.

PROS. COUNSEL: Didn't you? Are you selfish, Mr Leeson?

ROBERT: Not particularly, I think.

PROS. COUNSEL: Exactly. You are an administrative type, so you are not selfish. Professor King is a creative type, therefore it can be inferred——

ROBERT: But, no, it——

PROS. COUNSEL: Don't interrupt me; you are shielding your friend. So you are not aware that he is selfish? Let me remind you of just one episode. When that car accident occurred—the photographs of which are in the hands of the Jury—the only two people in your car were yourself and the Prisoner?

ROBERT: Yes.

PROS. COUNSEL: But it was the Prisoner who was driving the car?

ROBERT: Yes.

PROS. COUNSEL: *Your* car?

ROBERT: Yes, but we were taking it in turn.

PROS. COUNSEL: I did not ask you how you were taking it. The Prisoner was driving your car and he killed you?

ROBERT: Yes.

PROS. COUNSEL: And he promptly married your fiancée?

ROBERT: Yes.

PROS. COUNSEL: Thank you. That is all.

ROBERT: But please——

PROS. COUNSEL: That is all.

JERRY: Listen! It is not! Robert, just tell them——

JUDGE: Silence!

Prisoners at the Bar should be seen and not heard.

JERRY: My lord, I've got to be heard. Robert—the last witness—was right when he said we were two different types—him administrative, me creative. But I'm not ashamed of myself.

JUDGE: That means you're ashamed of *him.*

JERRY: But, my lord, it doesn't!

JUDGE: You have admitted you are two different types. So, if you're not ashamed of yourself, you must be ashamed of him. Believing as you do that people like yourself are so vastly superior to anyone else——

JERRY: But I don't believe that.

JUDGE: Your wife, when she was on the stand, made it only too clear that you do. Which no doubt is why you were so careless when driving your friend's car. The Jury I assume have by now studied the photographs and noted the extent of the damage.

JERRY: Robert, tell them! It was a skid! Tell them your tyres were worn out. If it was anyone's fault, it was yours, not mine, Robert. Tell the Judge that, Robert, tell him!

JUDGE: He can't tell me anything. He's dead.

CLERK OF THE COURT: Members of the Jury, the Prisoner at the Bar, Jeremiah King, is hereby charged with murder in that on the twentieth of May 1947 he——

JERRY: That's not the charge, that's not the charge, that's not the charge!

DEFENCE COUNSEL: My Lord, on behalf of my client, I submit that this case be dismissed.

JUDGE: On what ground, Mr Puller-Walker?

DEF. COUNSEL: I submit, my lord, that he is insane.

JUDGE: Really?

DEF. COUNSEL: Really, my lord.

JUDGE: Insane! Then he shouldn't be here. Have him removed at once.

USHER: Where to, my lord?

JUDGE: Where do you think, man!

[*The creaking door serves its purpose yet again.*]

BILL: Well, if it isn't Kingpin! We were all having bets who'd be the next.

JERRY: The next inmate, you mean?

BILL: No, Kingpin; the next boss. I'm surprised you accepted though. Thought you didn't fancy these administrative jobs.

JERRY: I didn't know I'd accepted.

BILL: Never mind; long live the Superintendent! You'll find this place is a scream—real little nest of mocking birds.

[*hums*] 'Laughing Hyena! Laughing Hyena!
  Who'll come a-laughing——'
It's a public service of course. Lead Kindly Gloom amid the encircling neons. Let me show you your office. No, just press this button so and ——

[*He presses the button and a smooth-sliding door reveals the best-appointed room in the asylum.*]

Posh, isn't it?

JERRY: Those damned mirrors again!

BILL: Yes, don't they tickle you pink! They have 'em in the wards too; makes the loonies feel young again. Talking of the loonies, you're

just in time for the charge list. Would you
like 'em brought in straightaway?

JERRY: I suppose so.

BILL: O.K., Sergeant! Bring in the first one.

SERGEANT: Coming, Mr Bryson.

[*He marches smartly up and clicks to attention.*]

BILL: Mr Superintendent, meet Mr Superfluous.

JERRY: What's this man charged with?

SERGEANT: Acute schizophrenia, not responsive to shock
treatment.

JERRY: I see. Have him put down.

SUPERFLUOUS: But, Mr Superintendent, I thought you could
cure me.

JERRY: Sorry, Mr Superfluous, I used to cure
people but now that I'm superintendent I
just can't spare the time. There's nothing
for it, I'm afraid: we must just have him put
down.

SERGEANT: Very good, Mr Superintendent. Take over,
wardress.

BILL: Next one's female.

WARDRESS: Stand to attention, you! Female indeed! I'll
female her!

BILL: Stow it, wardress.

EUNICE: Hiya, Jerry!

JERRY: Eunice! What are you doing in this bin?

EUNICE: They said I was a public nuisance.

JERRY: Surely not?

EUNICE: And that I was committing myself everywhere. Then the cop they send to arrest me
I kind of seduce him. And next they send me
some woman welfare worker and I kind of
seduce her too. And then they send me some
very important foreign guy and the two of us
get arrested for I guess they call it over-
exposure. That's him waiting in the doorway.

JERRY: I'll interview them together.

BILL: Come in, Doctor.

DOCTOR: Thank you. So we are meeting again. This is so nice, Professor.

JERRY: You think so, Doctor? Unveiled any statues lately?

DOCTOR: No statues, no, but this lady—I took upon me the liberty——

EUNICE: Ha! Ha! Statue of Liberty! That's what I call a pun. Real class pun, holding a flaming torch.

DOCTOR: I forget. You were holding a torch?

EUNICE: You big phoney, sure I was holding a torch! I'd be still right up there in New York Harbour, only *you* had to come and unveil me. Talk about strip tease! You should have seen the folk on the incoming liners——

DOCTOR: She is lying, there have been no liners. Only one punt on a river that is called Cam. You have been there too, Professor?

EUNICE: Yeah, he has been there too. But whenever I remember that cute little river, it's the other guy that I think of—what was his name—Robert. Gee, when I remember Robert——

JERRY: Shut up, Eunice! Bill?

BILL: Yes?

JERRY: What's your diagnosis of these two?

BILL: They're both paranoiacs, I'd say.

JERRY: I'd say so too. Have them put down.

EUNICE: Have us put where, Jerry?

JERRY: Down!

['*Going down*', *cries the* ELEVATOR BOY *yet again and the lift descends with the prisoners.*]

BILL: And this one is charged with delusions of grandeur.

JERRY: Is he? Why do you wear that black cap?
[*Pause.*]

Answer me.

JUDGE: Because I am a judge.

JERRY: But you're not judging anyone now.

JUDGE: Yes, I am.

JERRY: Who?

JUDGE: You, Jeremiah King. And I sentence you here and now to be hanged by the neck until——

JERRY: Give *me* that black cap! Sergeant!

SERGEANT: Here, Mr Superintendent.

JERRY: Have his lordship buried in quicklime.

SERGEANT: Very good, Mr Superintendent.

[*A pause while his lordship is removed.*]

JERRY: Any more to come?

SERGEANT: This black man.

JERRY: What's he charged with?

SERGEANT: Being black.

LEPER BOY: Black not mad, Bwana.

JERRY: Lookum, Leper Boy; black mighty mad. Black so mad not safe for white man. Black man foam at mouth, likeum own mammy far down in womb.

LEPER BOY: Bwana, listenum Leper Boy. Leper Boy not mad nohow. Leper Boy mighty good beater; not fear rhino, not fear buffalo, not fear leopard, not fear lion. Bwana ask Captain Vortrekker.

JERRY: Where's Vortrekker?

VORTREKKER: Here, man.

JERRY: How long have you known Leper Boy?

VORTREKKER: Since he came down from the trees.

JERRY: Would you say he's mad?

VORTREKKER: They're all mad. But this one's worse; he's a cripple.

BILL: Mens insana in corpore insano.

JERRY: Exactly, Bill. And as long as I'm head of this asylum I'm not going to have it full of lunatics.

LEPER BOY: Mercy, Bwana, mercy! Leper Boy mighty good Christian. Leper Boy learn God-palaver far down in Leper Hospital. Leper Boy makeum prayers for down in Garden of Eden.

VORTREKKER: Hear that, man? God, the lies they tell! He thinks he'll make you believe he's been to the Garden of Eden!

LEPER BOY: Leper Boy born in Garden of Eden. Beater for Father Adam. Father Adam send Leper Boy many times beatum beef. Beatum lion, beatum tiger, beatum unicorn, beatum snake. No, Leper Boy not mad.

SERGEANT: Mr Superintendent?

JERRY: Ah, there you are, Sergeant.

SERGEANT: Shall I put him down too?

VORTREKKER: You can't, man.

JERRY: Why not?

VORTREKKER: Take a look at him.

LEPER BOY: Mercy, Bwana, mercy!

VORTREKKER: Use your eyes, man. He's been put down already.

LEPER BOY: Mercy, Bwana, mercy.

VORTREKKER: And it's no good you saying that. That won't bring you to life again.

MARTHA: May I come in?

JERRY: Martha! What are you doing here? Not on the staff, are you?

MARTHA: No.

JERRY: You're visiting someone?

MARTHA: No.

JERRY: Then you heard I was here?

MARTHA: No. I'm on a charge too, Jerry.

JERRY: Who charged you?

MARTHA: You did.

JERRY: I did?

MARTHA: I was mad of course to marry you. Why have you got that black cap on?

JERRY: It is the cause, it is the cause, my soul.

LEPER BOY: Mercy, Bwana, mercy.

JERRY: Remove that body, Sergeant.

MARTHA: I ought to have gone on alone even though it meant Sally would be illegitimate. And afterwards, if I'd married anyone, the one person not to was you. You were driving that car, you see.

[*A cuckoo calls out of the past and, although* JERRY *is still in his dream, takes him back to a real scene in his past and* MARTHA'S. *The cuckoo keeps calling throughout.*]

BILL: Kingpin, I know she's your wife but—well, she's as bats as the rest of them.

JERRY: Shut up, Bill.

MARTHA: I told you at the time. I said: I shall never forgive you.

JERRY: That's not what you said, Martha.

MARTHA: But I also said: If you propose once again, I'll marry you for the child's sake. Only don't ever think I can love you.

JERRY: That's not what you said, darling.

MARTHA: It was the day after Robert's funeral. It was May, remember, there was a cuckoo calling. It was driving me mad, it went on so——

SERGEANT: Shall I have her put down now?

MARTHA: And the line kept running in my head: 'Cuckoo, cuckoo, oh bird of fear'—or is it 'word of fear'? 'Cuckoo, cuckoo, oh bird . . . oh word, . . . oh bird . . .'

JERRY: Shall we go indoors, Martha?

MARTHA: No, no, not indoors. Only I wish that would stop.

JERRY: The cuckoo?

MARTHA: Is it word of fear or bird of fear? Oh, it doesn't matter, it's fear.

The Administrator

JERRY: Martha, I wouldn't ask you again at this moment but . . . I'm thinking of the child you're going to have.

MARTHA: I'm thinking of it too. How's your arm?

JERRY: It will soon be out of the sling. But what about it, Martha?

MARTHA: I don't want to marry anyone ever. But this child of Robert's, apart from it being illegitimate how would I ever support it?

JERRY: I could solve those two questions, Martha.

MARTHA: I know you could but you couldn't solve me. I'd try to be a proper wife but . . . well, it wouldn't be fair to you. What's that Hans Andersen story about the little boy with the splinter of ice in his heart?

JERRY: Ice can be thawed, you know.

MARTHA: You're much too hopeful, Jerry. Remember what you told me a year ago when we were talking about cars?

JERRY: No.

MARTHA: 'One can always get out of a skid.'

JERRY: So you'll never forgive me?

MARTHA: Oh, I'm not as irrational as that. I know you didn't mean it—not even unconsciously. And you're good, you'd be good to the child.

JERRY: But you could never love me?

MARTHA: I don't even say that. I could in a way, I think, but——

[The cuckoo now speeds up like a machine gun.]

Listen to that bloody bird! Oh bird, oh word, of fear—— That line keeps running in my head.

[The cuckoo fades into the distance and the flashback gives way to the dream again.]

That line keeps running in my head. And I said to you: I shall never forgive you.

JERRY: That's not what you said, darling. But you

did say something about ice. Or was it an
iceberg?

BILL: Must have been an iceberg, Kingpin. Look
at the sea. It's full of 'em.

JERRY: I didn't know we were at sea.

[*The* SERGEANT *calls out from his post in the asylum.*]

SERGEANT: Goodbye, Mr Superintendent!

[*And* MARTHA *is left behind too.*]

MARTHA [*calling*]: Goodbye, Jerry!

BILL: Wake up, sir, wake up. We've just received
another ice signal. What shall we do about
it, sir?

JERRY: Why are you calling me 'sir', Bill?

BILL: You must be still dreaming, sir. My name's
not Bill; I'm your first officer, sir.

JERRY: Oh, so that's it, I was dreaming. All about
the month of May and cuckoos. Whereas in
fact, of course, it's March.

BILL: No, sir, if you'll excuse me, in fact it's the
fourteenth of April.

JERRY: Damned cold for April.

BILL: Temperature's down to thirty-one, sir.

JERRY: And the longitude?

BILL: 50.22 west, sir.

JERRY: Latitude?

BILL: 41.49 north, sir.

JERRY: As far north as that?

BILL: As far north as that, sir.

JERRY: Then what's that elephant doing swimming
over there to port? And all those—what are
they—kudu? If this is the North Atlantic,
how on earth did they get here?

BILL: I haven't the slightest idea, sir. All I know
is: they're drowning.

JERRY: Drowning, eh? Let's go up on the bridge.

BILL: But, sir, we *are* on the bridge. In our well-
appointed wheelhouse.

The Administrator

[*A low hum gradually increases and acquires a rhythm. These are the ship's engines and they also rise in pitch.*]

JERRY: Well-appointed wheelhouse? Sounds to me
more like Harwell. And looks to me more
like Harwell—all those panels of instruments.

[*The engines are still there but emerging through their noise are the tickings and clickings of instruments. Throughout the rest of this scene this medley of noise grows.*]

BILL: Yes, sir; the reactor's become critical.

JERRY: Why's that needle jumping about like that?

BILL: Indicates a ship in the vicinity.

JERRY: Big ship?

BILL: Biggest in the world.

JERRY: Bigger even than this one?

BILL: No, sir, but this is not a ship, sir. Have you
forgotten: you're in command of an iceberg!
'King is on his iceberg and a thousand miles
away.'

JERRY: So that's what it's come to. Point taken.
The Ice Age expects and I know where my
duty lies.
What's our speed?

BILL: Twenty-two and a half knots.

JERRY: Not fast enough.

BILL: If we go any faster, sir, we'll ram that ship.

JERRY: That's what I intend, you fool.

BILL: Very good, sir, but she's said to be unsink-
able. She's got sixteen watertight compart-
ments——

JERRY: I'll rip through the first five.

BILL: O.K., sir, but watch her; she's taking avoid-
ing action. Veering away to her port, sir.

JERRY: I'll soon see to that. You there at the wheel!
Starboard fifteen!

DOCTOR: Jawohl, Herr Capit—— Aye, aye, sir.

EUNICE [*calling*]: Attaboy, Captain King!

VORTREKKER [*calling*]: Get her in your sights, man!

The Administrator

JUDGE [*calling*]: Keep my black cap; you'll need it!

JERRY: Up twenty revolutions.

DOCTOR: Aye, aye, sir.

LEPER BOY [*calling*]: Mercy, Bwana, mercy!

BILL: Pile working, sir, pile working!

EUNICE: This should sure make news.

JERRY: News? This will make history. Ease helm.

DOCTOR: Aye, aye, sir.

[*The engines and the instruments rise to a crescendo. Both the noises and the ship go faster and faster.*]

BILL: Just look at those bloody dials!

LEPER BOY: Mercy, Bwana, mercy!

BILL: We can't miss her now; we'll hit her in the boiler rooms!

JERRY: Hit her? We'll sink her! Midships.

DOCTOR: Aye, aye, sir.

ROBERT [*calling*]: Jerry, this is Robert. Get out of that skid! This is Robert!

BILL: I can see her name, sir, now.

LEPER BOY: Mercy, Bwana, mercy!

JERRY: Stand by for the crash. What did you say?

BILL: I can see her name. The *Titanic*!

[*The collision sets off an alarm, as of a distorted telephone ringing. This resolves into a normal telephone.*]

MARTHA [*in some dream of her own*]: What's that all about? Must be Robert. To confirm that date on the river. No, we hadn't a date today. Robert is out of Cambridge.

[*JERRY, who has woken first, lifts the receiver.*]

TELEPHONE VOICE: Good morning. Rampart 6945? Your seven-thirty alarm call.

JERRY [*sleepily*]: Thank you.

[*He replaces the receiver.*]

Seven-thirty, darling.

MARTHA [*waking*]: What? Was that our alarm call?

JERRY: It was.

[*SALLY comes briskly in, as fresh as if she had not dreamt at all.*]

The Administrator

SALLY: Good morning, Mummy. Good morning, Daddy.

MARTHA: Sally, in your bare feet again!

SALLY: The telephone woke me up.

JERRY: That's a *non sequitur*. Sally, I hear you were dreaming about submarines.

SALLY: Yes? Why?

JERRY: A coincidence. I was dreaming at this moment about, er, something of the sort.

SALLY: My dream was really quite exciting. It came back, you know, and, Daddy, you were quite a hero in it.

JERRY: How do you mean it came back?

SALLY: Well, you know that I screamed and woke up Mummy——

JERRY: You woke me up too.

SALLY: I'm sorry. But anyway once I went to sleep again there I was back in the submarine. It was stuck on the bottom of the ocean and you said—you were the captain, you see——

JERRY: I see.

SALLY: You said: 'There's only one thing for it, we must open the escape hatch.' And Bill Bryson was there, he was some sort of junior officer and he said: 'I do admire a man that can take a decision.' Well, anyway, there was a lot I've forgotten but you opened this hatch thing yourself and we all shot up to the surface and the sun was shining and we all swam ashore and a big crowd came down to meet us with flags and drums and things and Mummy was there too, she was holding a big bunch of roses——

MARTHA: Roses?

SALLY: Then somebody shouted 'Three cheers for Captain King!' and then—well, that was about all.

The Administrator

[*There is quite a long pause.*]

JERRY: 'mm. So I made a good captain, did I?

SALLY: Super.

JERRY: Those escape hatches don't always work, you know.

MARTHA: Nothing works always but . . .

JERRY: What was it Bill Bryson said about me in your dream, Sally?

SALLY: 'I do admire a man who can take a decision'. He was right, wasn't he, Mummy?

MARTHA: Of course he was, Sally. We'd all admire Daddy if he took a decision, wouldn't we?

JERRY: In that case you can prepare to admire me now.

MARTHA: Oh, Jerry, you mean . . .? I always knew you'd come round. And I shan't have to nag any more, though I promised I wouldn't anyway. Oh, Jerry, how marvellous of you! Now we can all of us . . .

JERRY: Stop! I'm sorry, I shouldn't have put it like that: forget about the admiration. You see, darling, it's not your decision I've taken. I'm afraid this time it's my own.